Collins

DigiTech 2

Manasi Kashikar
Sneha Krishnan

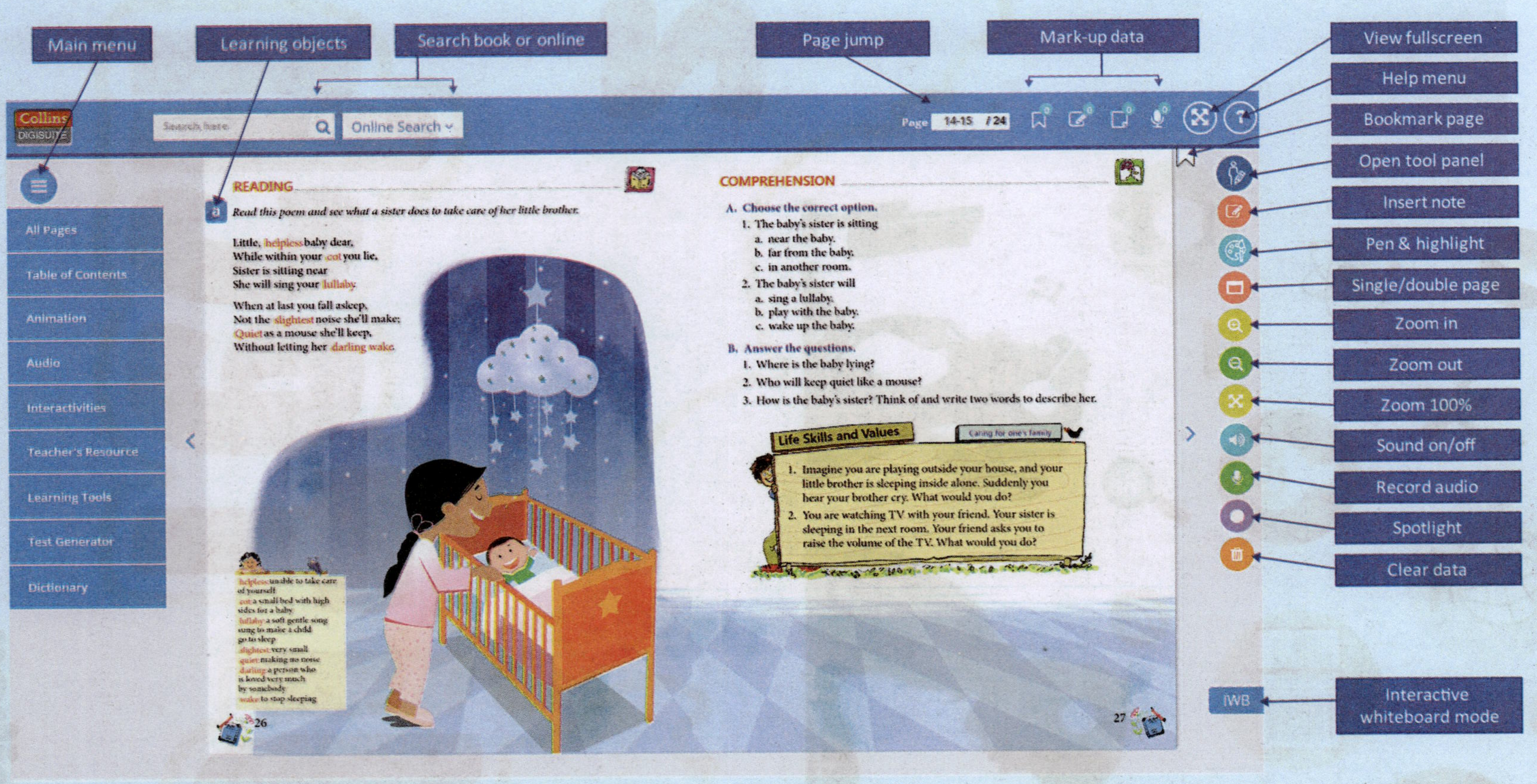

Student + Teacher			Teacher-only	
a animations	**ia** activities	**g** games	**lp** lesson plans	**tn** teacher's notes
ilt instructor-led tutorials	**w** worksheets	**v** videos	**w** worksheets	**ak** answer keys
	audio			

PREFACE

Over the last few decades, technology has touched almost all aspects of our lives. As technology continues to evolve more rapidly than ever, users are learning newer ways of harnessing the power of technology in their daily lives. In India, easy access to smartphones and affordable internet services have put the power of technology in the hands of millions.

In this backdrop, we believe, it is important for students to:

- ✓ Understand that technology is going to keep evolving. As citizens of the digital world that we all inhabit, keeping abreast of the latest advances is no longer optional, rather, it is an essential life skill.
- ✓ Appreciate that coding skills are as essential today as basic literacy and numeracy. This has been emphasized in the National Educational Policy of 2020 as well.
- ✓ Understand that technology is pervasive and they need to be able to comprehend its intersection with other disciplines. In other words, they need to learn to use technology as a tool to achieve a goal.
- ✓ Take control of regulating their usage and make constructive use of their access to computer devices.

While authoring this series, we have designed and presented the content with the intent of helping students in developing the skills described above. We have ensured that the topics are covered in a relatable manner and that the exercises are practical and applicable. The textbook along with its resources for teachers will enable them to deliver this subject effectively, while keeping the students engaged and interested.

In addition to the curriculum imperatives, we have included concepts as outlined in the National Education Policy 2020. Every grade has computational thinking–based practice problems that are aligned to Bloom's Taxonomy. Topics such as coding and app development have been given their due consideration as their relevance increases in the real world and while making career choices. Artificial intelligence has been woven into the chapters in an age-appropriate manner in the form of Fun with AI boxes, with the intent of enabling students to understand key concepts and applications of AI.

The series equips students with not only the skills required to excel in technology and make the most of it, but also exposes them to the practical applications of these in the world around them.

We would like to thank our intern Sejal Gupta in helping us shape the content.

KEY FEATURES

After reading this chapter, I will be able to:

- ✔ Discuss the different uses of computers.
- ✔ Explain the uses of a computer in schools and classrooms.
- ✔ State the uses of computers beyond the classroom.

Well-defined learning objectives that are mapped to the curriculum to help students identify the topics they will read about in the chapter

Activities and discussions based on real-life situations to set the context for what students are about to learn

Brainstorm and explore!

Ram loves working on the computer. These are the activities he wants to do on his computer today:

1. Finish his Maths project.
2. Make a new drawing.
3. Listen to his favourite songs.
4. Watch his favourite cartoon.

Ram starts after breakfast and finishes by lunch.

Who do you think will feel tired by lunch—Ram or his computer?

____

Soak up!

Never use a smart phone or a computer for 30 minutes to 1 hour before going to sleep. The light from the screen could affect the quality of sleep.

Additional information/facts about the topic being taught

Contextual meaning of difficult words

c. **Drag and drop:** We can move items around the screen by dragging and dropping them. It can be done by holding the left button and moving the mouse to drag the selected item. On leaving the left button, the item will get dropped where the cursor points.

drag and drop: select an item and move it to another location on the computer screen

Crank up!

A few output devices are also used to store data or information in the computer. These devices are known as storage devices. Examples of output devices that can be used as storage devices include CD, DVD and the pen drive.

Tips and shortcut tricks for the topics covered in the chapter to foster inquiry- and discovery-based learning

Clear up!

Open the MS Paint program. Select the Brushes tool. Write your name using different brushes and colours.

Brush up!

Can you draw a building and clouds on a computer? If yes, list the tools and shapes from MS Paint you will use to draw this.

____

____

Hands-on tasks for revision, based on the application of the concept taught

Short questions to reinforce the concept learned and promote competency-based learning

Recapitulates all the important points covered in the chapter

Today I learned!

- Electrical devices need power to work.
- A computer is an electronic device that accepts input from the user, processes it and then displays the output.
- A computer follows the IPO cycle. The full form of IPO is Input-Process-Output.
- Input is the data sent to a computer for processing.
- Doing a certain task or action on a given input is called processing.
- Output is the result that the computer gives back to the user after processing.
- Some of the advantages of a computer are large storage capacity, fast speed, automation, electronic presentation, teaching and learning, calculations and multitasking.
- Pollution, health ill-effects, virus attacks, cybercrime and lack of emotions are some of the disadvantages of a computer.

Revision exercises comprising a blend of both objective and long-answer questions, including both fact- and application-based questions in a variety of formats

Revise and polish!

Learning Skills

1. Tick (✓) the correct answer.

a. Who gives input to a computer?

(i) User ☐ (ii) Printer ☐

(iii) Monitor ☐ (iv) Process ☐

b. What turns an input into an output?

(i) Keyboard ☐ (ii) Process ☐

(iii) User ☐ (iv) Mouse ☐

Lab Activities

Experiential Learning

Look at a computer in your computer lab. Write the names of all the input and output devices you see there.

a. Input devices ____________________

b. Output devices ____________________

Based on the practical application of the concepts taught to enhance comprehension and provide opportunities for peer tutoring

Practical applications of the concepts covered to help analyse and understand real-world situations, with some extra effort put into research and information gathering

Projects

1. Plant a seed and click pictures of a growing plant every week for 10 weeks. At the end of 10 weeks, arrange these pictures week-wise on your computer and see the progress.

Congratulations! You just did what scientists do to record information and note down their analysis. Working with information properly is a very important use of computers.

2. List three additional places where computers are used. Collect pictures of these places.

Worksheet 1 (Chapters 1 and 2)

Art Integration

Learning Skills

1. Colour the features of computers in red and those of humans in blue.

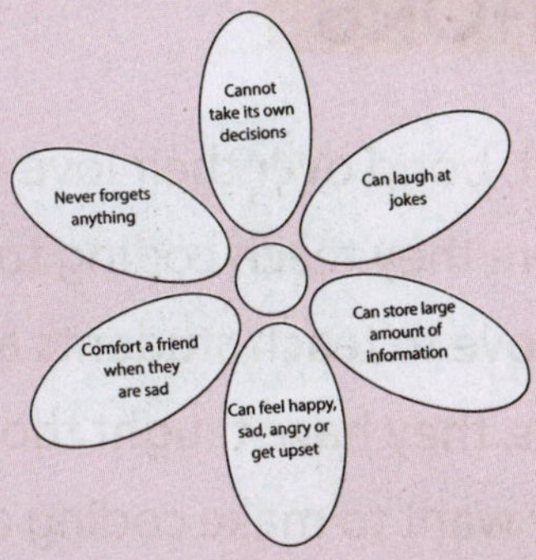

Chapter-based revision worksheets focused on competency-based learning and one dedicated worksheet on developing computational thinking through playing games and problem-solving

NEP IN DIGI TECH

These are some of the key skills that you will see occurring throughout the books at various stages.

21st Century Skills

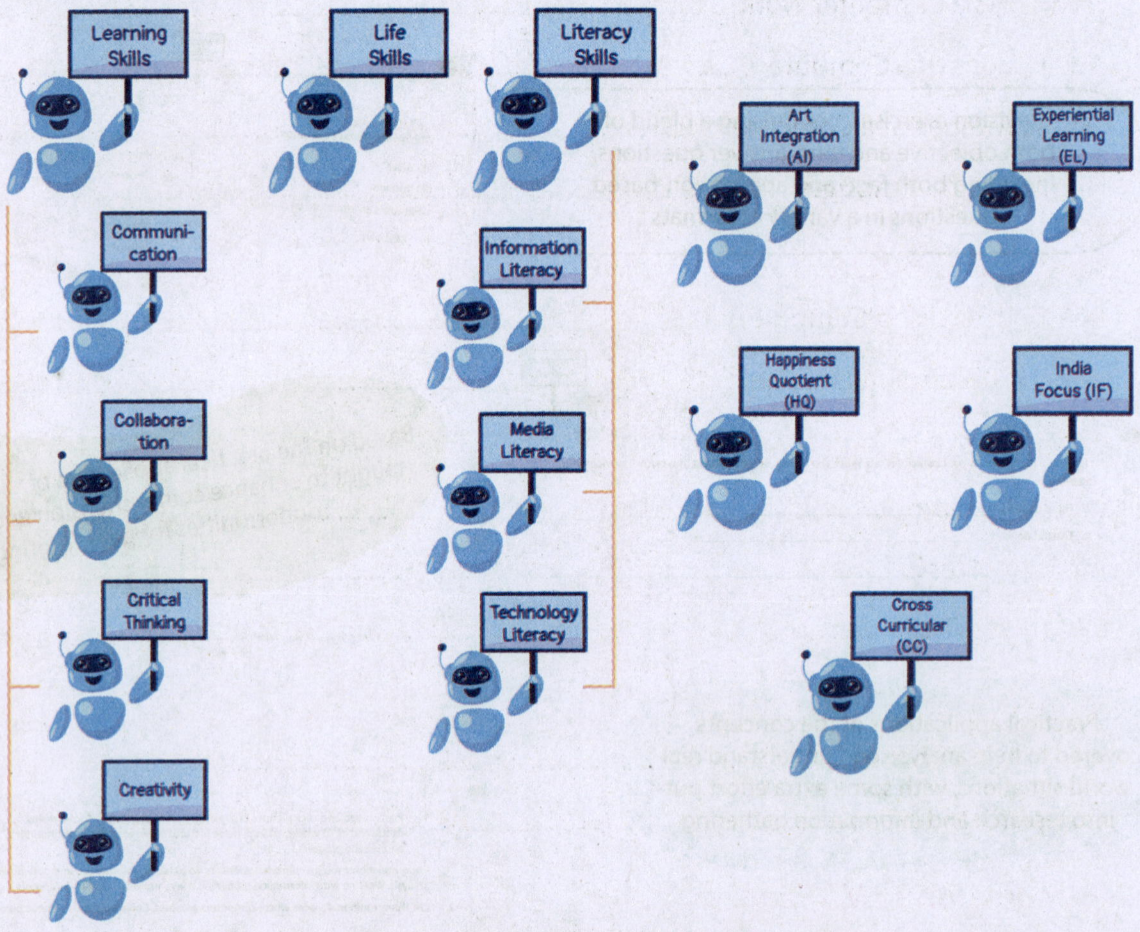

ABOUT THE AUTHORS

Sneha Krishnan and **Manasi Kashikar**, techies at heart, bond over their love of coding. They are co-founders of the company *MindChamp* where they teach coding to school students using fun, activity-based learning. They both love to teach students and that reflects in their work. Together with a team of educators, they have taught thousands of students to create computer games and websites. They want to make coding accessible to young students as well, so they are better equipped for the future.

CONTENTS

Chapter 1

Computer—An Electronic Device

After reading this chapter, I will be able to:

- ✔ Describe why a computer is an electronic device.
- ✔ Explain the IPO cycle.
- ✔ Describe the advantages and disadvantages of a computer.
- ✔ Compare a human and a computer in their ways of working.

Brainstorm and explore!

Information Literacy

Ram loves working on the computer. These are the activities he wants to do on his computer today:

1. Finish his Maths project.
2. Make a new drawing.
3. Listen to his favourite songs.
4. Watch his favourite cartoon.

Ram starts after breakfast and finishes by lunch.

Who do you think will feel tired by lunch—Ram or his computer?

____

A computer is a machine that can perform a variety of tasks. We can tell a computer what we want it to do. For example, Ram used his computer to make a drawing, listen to songs and watch a cartoon.

What are Electrical and Electronic Devices?

We know that machines help us do difficult tasks with less effort. Some machines can do only one task. For example, a fan can only cool the room or a pair of scissors can be used only to cut things.

Some machines require power to work. Those machines that require power to work are called **electrical devices**.

For example, an iron or a television needs to be connected to a power source, such as battery or electricity, to run. Electrical machines can perform only one task. They cannot be used to store or process information.

Fig. 1.1 | *Electrical devices*

A computer is an **electronic device**. It is made up of electronic parts. A computer uses electricity to run. It can be used to process data and give results. A computer can be used to perform different tasks. A computer uses electricity to store and process information. We will learn more about this in later classes.

For example, a computer can be used to play games, watch cartoons, make drawings, listen to music, etc.

Fig. 1.2 | *Many uses of computers*

How Does a Computer Work?

In a computer, the user sends information. This information is called the input. **Input** can include instructions and information. **Output** is the information given by the computer to the user. Let us learn more about how a computer works.

Data is the information processed by or stored in a computer. This information may be in the form of text documents, images, audio clips, software programs or other types of data.

We know that computers cannot work on their own. We need to tell the computer what to do. Computers take the input from the users, process the input as per the instructions and give the output to the users. This order of steps is known as the **IPO cycle**. IPO stands for Input-Process-Output.

Soak up!

We use the IPO cycle in our daily life as well. For example, we put our dirty clothes in a washing machine (input). The machine washes and dries our clothes (process). We get clean clothes (output).

information: facts about someone or something

instructions: clear and detailed information on how to do something

To do any work on the computer, we have to follow the IPO cycle. The computer *takes* the input, *processes* it and *gives* the output.

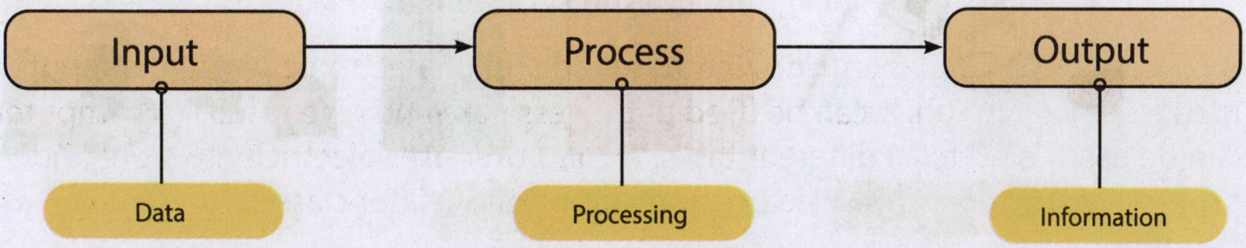

Fig. 1.3 | *The IPO cycle*

Any data sent to a computer for processing is called **input**. For example, we use a keyboard to enter data into a computer.

Process is doing a certain task or action. This takes place in the CPU. Thus, the CPU is known as the brain of the computer.

The result that computer gives back to the user after processing is called **output**. For example, the computer displays the result of processing using the monitor.

So, when a video is played, three things happen inside the CPU of the computer. This is shown in Fig. 1.4.

Input: Clicking on the play button

Process: Buffering

Output: The video playing

Fig. 1.4 | *Input, processing and output while playing a video*

Clear up!

Look at the following images. Write 'I' for an input activity, 'P' for a process and 'O' for an output activity.

1.

2.

Advantages of a Computer

A computer helps us in many ways. Some of the advantages of computers are given here:

- **Storage Capacity**: A computer can store large amounts of data in the form of documents, images, videos, etc.

Fig. 1.5 | *Computers have a lot of storage capacity*

Fig. 1.6 | *Computers never get tired*

- **Non-stop Working**: A computer never gets tired. It can work without taking rest.

- **Speed**: A computer can process the input at a very fast speed. It can give accurate results in a very short span of time.

Fig. 1.7 | *Computers are very fast*

Technology Literacy

Crank up!

Take help of your teacher. Open the Calculator application on the computer. Carry out the following operations:

a. 1 + 1

b. 342830923 + 129401930

For both the additions, note the time your computer takes to give the result.

Did you notice that the computer took the same time to do the both the additions? This is because the computer can do calculations very quickly.

Fig. 1.8 | *Computers are automatic*

- **Automation**: Computers can be set up to perform the same task repeatedly, without human intervention. This is called automation. Automation saves both time and effort for humans.

  Thus, it takes less effort to do the same job using a computer.

Soak up!

Some examples of automation are given below:

Human effort	Automation
Drawing 50 posters by hand	Designing a poster and printing 50 copies
The teacher sending holiday notice to every parent, individually	The teacher sending a single email with a holiday notice to all the parents in one click

- **Electronic Presentation**: A computer can display information in the form of images, videos and text.

Fig. 1.9 | *Computers can display information*

Fig. 1.10 | *Computers are used for learning and teaching*

- **Teaching and Learning**: A computer can store a vast amount of data. It can also display the data at the click of a button. Thus, computers are very useful in classrooms for learning and teaching.

- **Multitasking**: A computer can do many things at the same time. For example, we can make a drawing while listening to our favourite songs.

Fig. 1.11 | *Computers can do multitasking*

Disadvantages of a Computer

Here are some disadvantages of using a computer:

- **Impact on Environment**: When computers and other electronics get old, we replace them with new devices. All of the old devices that get thrown away are called digital waste. They harm the environment in many ways. We should be careful about the devices we throw away. Reusing and recycling help us to reduce the impact of digital waste on the environment.

Fig. 1.12 | *Electronic waste affects the environment*

- **Health Effects**: If we overuse or misuse computers, our health can get affected. Sitting in an incorrect posture while using a computer can lead to body ache.

Fig. 1.13 | *Incorrect posture leads to bad health*

Fig. 1.14 | *Virus attacks lead to data loss*

- **Virus Attacks**: A virus can attack a computer at the time of data transfer. We may lose our data due to a virus attack.

Fig. 1.15 | *Data protection is at risk while using a computer*

- **Cybercrimes**: We use the internet to make video calls or shop online. Someone can misuse our data (like passwords) to access our details and harm us. This is called cybercrime.

Fig. 1.16 | *Computers cannot take decisions on their own*

- **Decisions**: A computer cannot take decisions on its own. It needs instructions to work.

Fig. 1.17 | *Computers do not have feelings*

- **Feelings and Emotions**: Unlike humans, computers lack emotions and feelings.

Soak up!

Never use a smart phone or a computer for 30 minutes to 1 hour before going to sleep. The light from the screen could affect the quality of sleep.

Brush up!

Tick (✓) the correct posture and cross (X) the incorrect posture.

Humans and Computers

A computer is a smart machine. Let us discuss some of its features that make it a smart machine. Table 1.1 shows the differences between humans and computers.

Table 1.1 | *Humans vs computers*

Humans	Computers
Humans might make mistakes while solving sums.	A computer never makes mistakes. It always shows us the correct answer.
Humans are slow. They take time in doing calculations.	A computer works much faster than humans. It can perform calculations at a very fast speed.
Humans feel tired.	A computer never gets tired. It can work non-stop without taking rest.
Humans cannot remember everything all the time.	A computer can be used to store a lot of information. It never forgets anything.
Humans can take their own decisions.	A computer needs instructions to work. It cannot take its own decisions.
Humans feel emotions, such as happiness, sadness or anger.	A computer lacks emotions.

Brush up!

Match the following tasks with humans or computers.

I can solve sums quickly.

I can water the plants.

I remember everything.

I can make a sandwich.

I can book tickets.

I can decide what to do.

Today I learned!

- Electrical devices need power to work.
- A computer is an electronic device that accepts input from the user, processes it and then displays the output.
- A computer follows the IPO cycle. The full form of IPO is Input-Process-Output.
- Input is the data sent to a computer for processing.
- Doing a certain task or action on a given input is called processing.
- Output is the result that the computer gives back to the user after processing.
- Some of the advantages of a computer are large storage capacity, fast speed, automation, electronic presentation, teaching and learning, calculations and multitasking.
- Pollution, health ill-effects, virus attacks, cybercrime and lack of emotions are some of the disadvantages of a computer.

Revise and polish!

Learning Skills

1. Tick (✓) the correct answer.

a. Who gives input to a computer?

(i) User ☐ (ii) Printer ☐

(iii) Monitor ☐ (iv) Process ☐

b. What turns an input into an output?

(ii) Keyboard ☐ (iii) Process ☐

(i) User ☐ (ii) Mouse ☐

c. Which of the following is not an advantage of a computer?

(i) Storage capacity ☐ (ii) Speed ☐

(iii) Automation ☐ (iv) Cybercrimes ☐

d. What can attack a computer at the time of data transfer?

(i) Health effects ☐ (ii) Environment ☐

(iii) Output ☐ (iv) Virus attacks ☐

e. Which of the following is not a feature of humans?

(i) Feelings ☐ (ii) Emotions ☐

(iii) Tiredness ☐ (iv) Processing speed ☐

2. Fill in the blanks using the given words.

data electricity computer CPU Output

a. IPO stands for Input-Process-_____________.

b. A computer processes data in the _____________.

c. A computer runs on _____________.

d. A _____________ saves time and effort for repetitive tasks.

e. We may lose our _____________ due to a virus attack.

3. State whether the following statements are true (T) or false (F).

a. Input is taken from the monitor. ☐

b. A computer is an electronic device. ☐

c. We watch television without connecting it to a power source. ☐

d. Virus is very useful for a computer. ☐

e. Processing means doing a certain action. ☐

4. Match the following.

a.	Runs on a battery	(i)	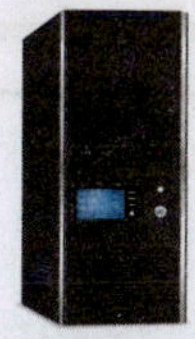
b.	Runs on electricity	(ii)	
c.	Brain of the computer	(iii)	
d.	Displays output	(iv)	
e.	Takes input	(v)	

5. Read the following activities carefully. Tick (✓) if it is an example of automation; else, cross (✕) it.

a. Making notes in your notebook

☐

b. Sharing your notes via email with all your friends

☐

c. Making a greeting card on your computer

☐

d. Eating a piece of chocolate

☐

6. Colour the thing that runs on battery.

Experiential Learning

Lab Activities

1. Identify and name a few electronic devices used at home and school.
2. Share more examples from real life to show that the IPO cycle is used in everyday tasks.

Chapter

2

Role of Computers

After reading this chapter, I will be able to:

- ✔ Discuss the different uses of computers.
- ✔ Explain the uses of a computer in schools and classrooms.
- ✔ State the uses of computers beyond the classroom.

Brainstorm and explore!

Learning Skills

Discuss the uses of computers learned in the previous class.
Now, match the following.

<table>
<tr><td>1. </td><td>a. Tracking planes</td></tr>
<tr><td>2. </td><td>b. Speaking to relatives on a video call</td></tr>
<tr><td>3. </td><td>c. Learning from videos</td></tr>
</table>

A computer is a smart device. We use it for many activities today at home and other places. Most schools, offices and shops use computers. We can draw and colour pictures, play games, make notes, watch cartoons, listen to music and solve sums on a computer.

Reasons for Using Computers at Different Places

Computers are used at almost all places. Let us learn the reasons for using computers at different places.

Computers can **store a lot of information**. This feature makes them very useful in places, such as schools, offices, banks, hospitals, and shops.

Computers in Schools

Computers are used in schools for teaching and learning. Teachers use computers to teach in the classrooms. Students use computers to learn. Schools also use computers to keep a record of all students and teachers.

Fig. 2.1 | *Computers in schools*

Inside the Classroom

Teachers and students use computers for teaching and learning. Here are some of the uses of a computer in a classroom:

- Multimedia and animations make it easy-to-teach and learn new concepts.
- Audio helps learn a new language.

multimedia: computer programs and products which involve sound, pictures, and film, as well as text

animation: a film in which drawings or puppets appear to move

Teachers use computers to:

- Conduct online classes and tests
- Create lesson plans and assignments
- Communicate with parents using emails

Fig. 2.2 | *Teacher using computers*

- Keep record of students' performance and attendance
- Access resources outside textbooks, such as e-books, internet-based resources, etc.

Soak up!

There are special applications that teachers use for teaching, learning and tracking the performance of students. It also helps them connect with parents and share the progress report of students. These applications are called learning management systems (LMS).

Outside the Classroom

Computers are useful in schools beyond the classroom as well. Schools use computers to collect fees and keep track of students, teachers and the staff.

Brush up!

Discuss with your teacher and give two additional uses of computers in your school.

____

____

Computers in Offices

- Computers are used to store data and handle communication in offices.
- Officers use computers to type and print project reports.
- Computers are used to maintain office records.
- Computers are used to store important information.
- Computers are used to send and receive messages and emails.

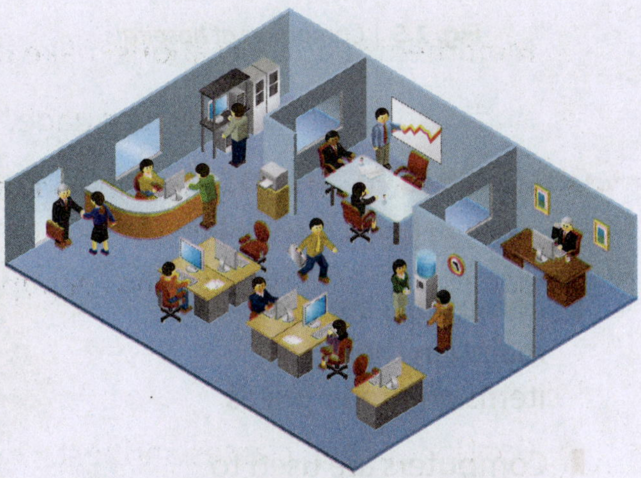

Fig. 2.3 | *Computers in offices*

Computers at Banks

- Computers help in keeping records of bank accounts.
- Computers help in printing statements.
- Computers help in taking out money from the ATM (Automated Teller Machine).

Fig. 2.4 | *Computers at banks*

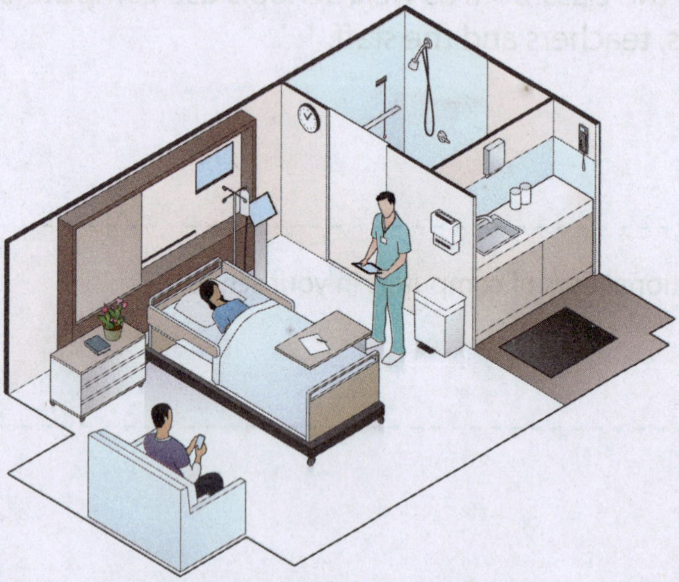

Fig. 2.5 | *Computers at hospitals*

Computers at Hospitals

- Computers are used for maintaining the records of patients.
- Doctors use computers to diagnose a patient's illness.
- Computers help in preparing medical reports.

Computers at Shops/Supermarkets/Hotels

- Computers are used to maintain the list of items and their prices.
- Computers are used to make and print bills.

Fig. 2.6 | *Computers at shops*

Computers at Home

Computers are very good for **entertainment and communication**. For this reason, we use computers at homes.

- Our elders use computers for online shopping.
- We can watch movies and listen to music on a computer.
- We can play games on a computer.
- We can talk to people staying far away from us.

Fig. 2.7 | *Computers at home*

Computers at Railway Stations and Airports

Computers help us **access real-time information.** This makes them useful at Railway stations and Airports.

- Computers are used to book tickets for trains and flights.
- We can track trains and flights using computers.

Fig. 2.8 | *Computers at airports*

Computers for Art, Design and Architecture

Computers can be used to **create difficult designs and plans quickly**. This makes them helpful in the fields of Arts, Design and Architecture.

- A computer helps architects in designing homes and buildings.
- A computer helps engineers in designing bikes, cars, airplanes and other machines.

architect: a person who designs buildings

engineer: a person who designs, constructs and maintains engines and machines or structures, such as roads, railways and bridges

Fig. 2.9 | *Computers for designing*

Computers for Space and Research

Computers can **perform high-speed complex calculations**. This feature makes them useful in the fields of Space and Research.

- Scientists study weather conditions with the help of computers.
- Computers help in launching rockets.
- Computers help scientists in designing and controlling robots.

Fig. 2.10 | *Computers in research*

Clear up!

Write two ways in which computers are helpful to the following people.

1. 

Doctor

2. 

Engineer

3. 

Architect

4. 

Bank employee

5. 

Scientist

Impact of Computers

Computers have made teaching and learning smarter in many ways. Some of these are discussed here:

1. They have enhanced classroom learning experience. Computers provide following supplements to enhance learning:
   a. Audiovisual aids, such as animations, videos, etc.
   b. E-books to make teaching and learning interactive and engaging
   c. Easy concept revision
   d. Online tests to support learning without wasting paper
2. Computers have made online teaching possible through virtual classrooms.
3. Anytime, anywhere learning is available through specialized learning and teaching apps.

Fig. 2.11 | *Impact of computers in teaching and learning*

Today I learned!

- We use a computer for many activities today at home and other places.
- Computers can store a lot of information. This feature makes them very useful in places, such as schools, offices, banks, hospitals, and shops.
- Computers are very good for entertainment and communication. For this reason, we use computers at homes.
- Computers help us access real-time information. This feature makes them useful at railway stations and airports.
- Computers can be used to create difficult designs and plans quickly. This feature makes them helpful in the fields of Arts, Design and Architecture.
- Computers can perform high-speed complex calculations. This feature makes them useful in the fields of Space and Research.
- Computers have a great impact on everyday learning and teaching.

Revise and polish!

Learning Skills

1. Tick (✓) the correct answer.

a. Which of the following features of computers makes them useful in the classroom?

(i) Computers can be connected to the internet. ☐

(ii) Computers allow us to access multimedia resources. ☐

(iii) Computers have a good storage capacity. ☐

(iv) All of the above. ☐

b. Why are computers used in airports?

(i) Tracking airplanes ☐ (ii) Sending report cards to parents ☐

(iii) Emailing homework to students ☐ (iv) Taking online tests ☐

c. Which place uses computers to maintain a record of patients?

(i) Banks ☐ (ii) Hospitals ☐

(iii) Home ☐ (iv) Office ☐

d. How are the computers used outside the classroom in a school?

(i) To understand concepts, when connected to a projector ☐

(ii) To send robots to Mars ☐

(iii) To maintain records of teachers and staff ☐

(iv) To track planes and trains ☐

e. Why are computers used in Space and Research?

(i) To keep records of employees ☐ (ii) To mix tunes to create a song ☐

(iii) To perform high-speed calculations ☐ (iv) To cook food ☐

2. Fill in the blanks using the given words.

Hospitals teach data computers entertainment

a. Scientists use computers to record ____________.

b. Teachers use computers to ____________.

c. Computers are used at home for ____________.

d. ____________ use computers to maintain record of patients.

e. Architects design homes and buildings using ____________.

3. **State whether the following statements are true (T) or false (F).**

a. Scientists study weather conditions with the help of computers. ☐

b. Computers are used at banks to play games. ☐

c. Computers are used for maintaining the records of patients. ☐

d. Computers help us access real-time information. ☐

e. Computers do not impact learning and teaching. ☐

4. **Read the following uses of computers. Write down the place where they are used and by whom.**

Use	Place	By Whom
a. Watch educational videos to understand concepts better		
b. Make and print bills		
c. Online shopping		
d. Book train tickets		
e. Launch rockets		

5. **Give two uses of computers at the following places.**

a. Classrooms

____

____

b. Offices

____

____

c. Hospitals

____

____

d. Research labs

____

____

6. **On the left, write three things a computer can do. On the right, write down three things that a computer cannot do.**

a.

b.

c.

d.

e.

f.

Projects

1. Plant a seed and click pictures of a growing plant every week for 10 weeks. At the end of 10 weeks, arrange these pictures week-wise on your computer and see the progress.

   Congratulations! You just did what scientists do to record information and note down their analysis. Working with information properly is a very important use of computers.

2. List three additional places where computers are used. Collect pictures of these places.

Chapter
3

Input and Output Devices

After reading this chapter, I will be able to:

- ✔ Define input and output devices.
- ✔ Identify different input and output devices.
- ✔ State the functions of each device.

Brainstorm and explore!

Technology Literacy

Name these devices. What are they used for?

a.

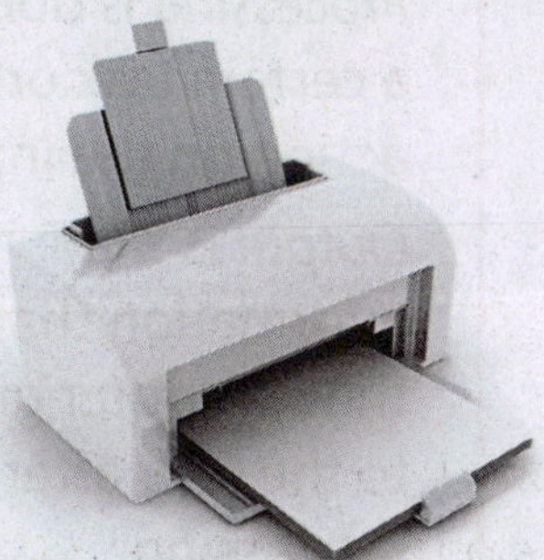

b.

c.

Input and Output

Imagine your Maths teacher says that you get to ask questions to your friends! When your turn comes, you ask your friend a very simple question: What is the sum of 1 and 2?

You asking | *Your friend's brain doing the maths* | *Your friend giving the answer*

Fig. 3.1 | *Example of input, processing and output*

You are asking your friend to add two numbers. This means he is taking information. This is known as **input**.

Your friend's brain does the work, that is, to add 1 and 2. This is known as **processing**.

Finally, your friend gives you the answer. This is the result of the question. It is known as **output**.

Similarly, we give input to the computer (1 + 2), the computer processes the input and gives us the output (3).

> *Input* is information given to a computer. *Processing* is doing a certain task or action on the input. *Output* is the information that the computer gives to the user after processing.

Brush up!

Which part of the computer does the processing? ____________

Hint: It is also called the brain of computer.

Special parts of a computer help us give the input to the computer and receive the output. These are called input devices and output devices. Now, let us learn about input and output devices.

Input Devices

A hardware device that sends input to a computer is called an input device. It is used by the user to give information to the computer.

We know that:

- a **keyboard** is used for typing.
- a **mouse** is used for clicking and selecting.
- a **scanner** is used to read images in the computer.

Input devices give information or input to the computer.

All of these devices are used to give information to the computer. These are examples of input devices. We will now learn about some more input devices.

Microphone

A microphone is an input device. It is used to record audio into the computer or speak to other users via computers.

Fig. 3.2 | *Microphone*

Joystick

Fig. 3.3 | *Joystick*

Joystick is an input device. It is used to play video games.

Webcam

A webcam is an input device. It is used to make video calls and take pictures. In desktop computers, it is placed above the monitors for making calls.

Fig. 3.4 | *Webcam*

Brush up!

Here are a few input devices. What type of input does each device provide? Write it here.

1. Keyboard ______________________
2. Scanner ______________________
3. Webcam ______________________
4. Microphone ______________________

Output Devices

The input is processed by the CPU. The computer shows the output to the user.

The hardware device that shows the result to the user is called an output device.

We know that:

- a **monitor** is used to watch movies.
- a **printer** is used to take printouts.
- a **speaker** is used to listen to songs.

Output devices show or give the result to the user.

All of these devices are used to give the result to the user. These are examples of output devices. We will now learn about some more output devices.

Headphones

Headphones are a pair of small speakers used for listening to sound without disturbing others. They are safe to use, as long as you do not keep them at a high volume.

Fig. 3.5 | *Headphones*

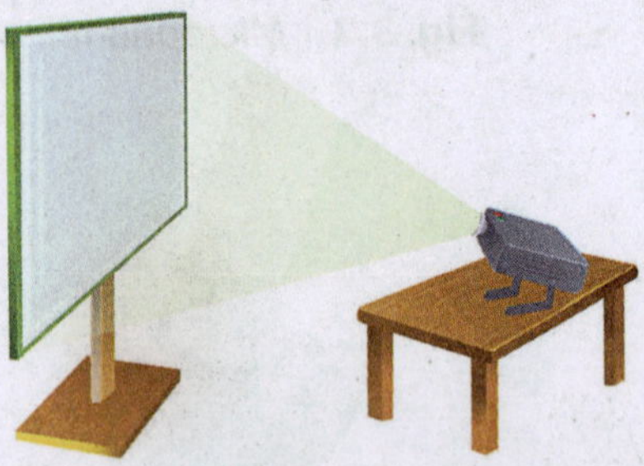

Fig. 3.6 | *Projector*

Projector

A projector is a device that projects an image onto a large surface. It is mostly used while giving presentations or playing movies in a theatre.

Plotter

A plotter is a device used for printing big drawings. It uses a pen, pencil or marker to print these drawings.

Fig. 3.7 | *Plotter*

Technology Literacy

Crank up!

A few output devices are also used to store data or information in the computer. These devices are known as storage devices. Examples of output devices that can be used as storage devices include CD, DVD and the pen drive.

Brush up!

Why is a monitor both an input and an output device?

Hint: Think about working of the touchscreens.

Soak up!

Certain devices that give and take information from the computer are called input-output or I/O devices.
For example, touchscreen, monitors, headphones with mic, etc.

Clear up!

Match the following.

a. Keyboard	b. Mouse	c. CPU	d. Monitor	e. Printer
(i) 	(ii) 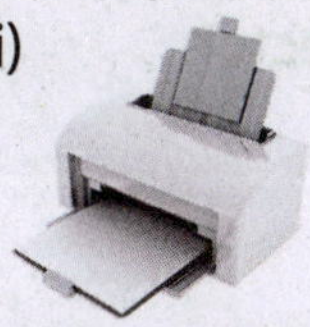	(iii) 	(iv) 	(v) 

Today I learned!

- Input is the information given to a computer.
- Processing is doing a certain task or action based on the input.
- Output is the information that the computer gives to the user after processing.
- A hardware device that provides input to the computer is called an input device. Keyboard, mouse, scanner, microphone, joystick and webcam are some input devices.
- A hardware device that shows the output to the user is called an output device. Monitor, speakers, printer, headphones, projector and plotter are some output devices.

Revise and polish!

Learning Skills

1. Tick (✓) the correct answer.

a. Which of the following is a use of the microphone?

(i) Typing a letter ☐ (ii) Printing a letter ☐

(iii) Reading a letter ☐ (iv) Recording audio of a letter ☐

b. Which input device is used to make video calls?

(i) Keyboard ☐ (ii) Webcam ☐

(iii) Printer ☐ (iv) Mouse ☐

c. Which of the following is not an output device?

(i) Keyboard ☐ (ii) Monitor ☐

(iii) Plotter ☐ (iv) Projector ☐

d. Why do we use a joystick?

(i) Colouring a picture ☐ (ii) Taking print of a picture ☐

(ii) Playing games ☐ (iv) Recording audio ☐

e. Which output devices do we use to make presentations?

(i) Headphones ☐ (ii) Joystick ☐

(iii) Plotter ☐ (iv) Projector ☐

2. Fill in the blanks using the given words.

Webcam Output Input I/O Printer

a. ____________ is an output device.

b. ____________ devices are used to give instructions to a computer.

c. The full form of ____________ is Input/Output.

d. ____________ is the data sent by the computer to the user.

e. ____________ is used to make video calls.

3. State whether the following statements are true (T) or false (F).

a. Any information given to a computer for processing is called input. ☐

b. Computers process the input to give the output. ☐

c. Plotter is an input device. ☐

d. Keyboard can also be used as an output device. ☐

e. Input devices are used to give information to the user. ☐

4. Name the input or output devices that you need in the following situations.

a. To play games ____________

b. To type a story ____________

c. To print the story you have just typed ____________

d. To listen to a story on the computer ____________

e. To see the people far away from us ____________

5. Colour and label all the input devices in the picture.

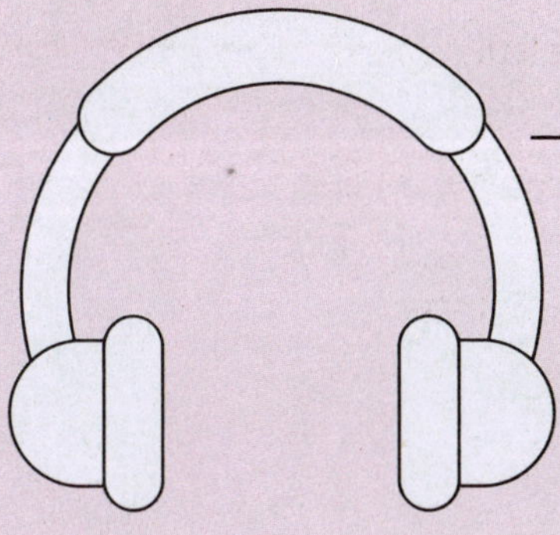
____

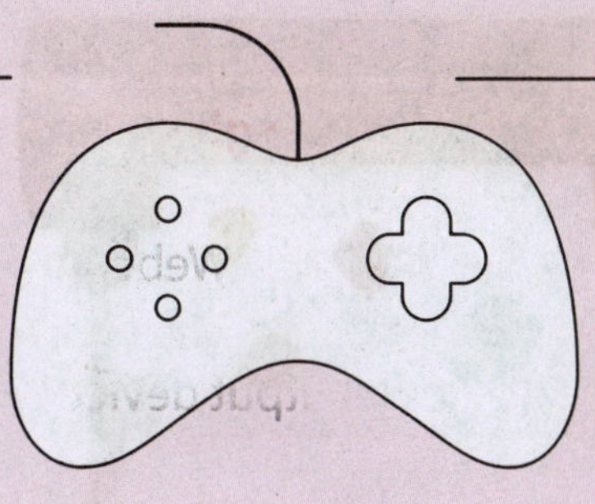
____

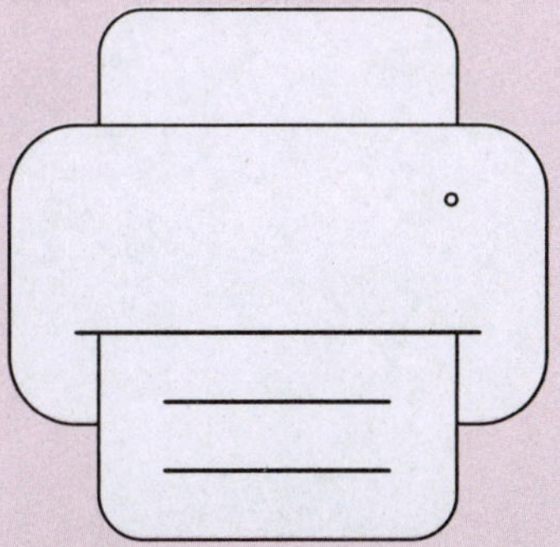
____

____

6. Identify the following devices as input or output devices and write their use.

	Device	Input/Output Device	Uses
a.			
b.			
c.			
d.			
e.			

Lab Activity

Experiential Learning

Look at a computer in your computer lab. Write the names of all the input and output devices you see there.

a. Input devices ______________________

b. Output devices ______________________

Group Activity

Collaboration

Make groups of four children. Each child will explain the different devices and their functions to the others in the group.

Think and Answer

Critical Thinking

Even our mobile phone is a computer. Can you think and tell which input device we use in our mobile phones?

____

____

____

____

Project

Draw and colour any two devices of your choice.

Chapter
4

More About Keyboard and Mouse

After reading this chapter, I will be able to:

- ✔ Identify and use special keys.
- ✔ Use certain keys in combinations.
- ✔ Describe the functions of the different types of keys.
- ✔ Identify different activities performed on a mouse.

Brainstorm and explore!

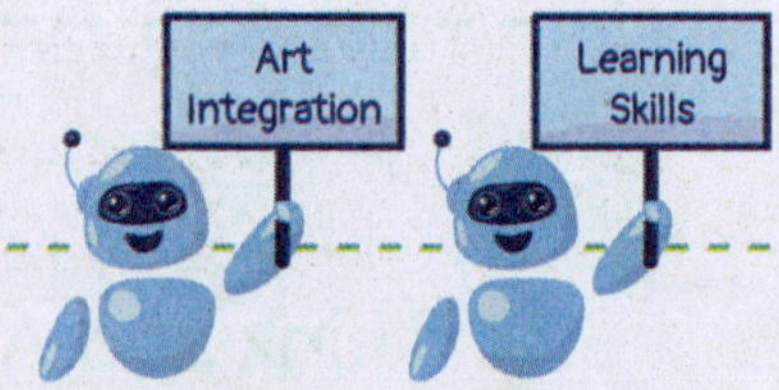

Use the following colours to label the different keys of the keyboard:

Alphabet keys: Pink	**Enter keys**: Red	**Number keys**: Green	**Arrow keys**: Orange	**Num Lock key**: Yellow

Mouse and keyboard are the main parts of a desktop computer. Let us discuss more about these parts in detail.

Keys on a Keyboard

A keyboard is used to type in a computer. It has many buttons called keys. We can type letters and numbers with the help of these keys.

Apart from letter and number keys, a keyboard has many other keys. These additional keys are used for special functions. The keys on a keyboard can be divided mainly into five types:

Fig. 4.1 | *Keys on a keyboard*

1. **Main typing keys**: These have the following keys:
   a. Alphabet keys (letters from A – Z)
   b. Number keys (numbers from 0 – 9)
   c. Punctuation keys (., ;, :, ", etc.)
   d. Symbol keys (+, –, *, &, %, etc.)
   e. Control keys (Ctrl, Alt, Windows logo key and Esc)
2. **Navigation keys**: These keys are used for moving on the screen. Page Up, Page Down, Delete, Home, End and Insert keys are the navigation keys.
3. **Numeric keypad**: It is located on right side of the keyboard. Numeric keypad consists of numbers (0–9) and mathematical operators, such as addition (+), subtraction (–), multiplication (*) and division (/).
4. **Function keys**: These keys are labeled as F1, F2, F3, and so on, up to F12. They perform specific tasks.
5. **Arrow keys**: Arrow keys are used to move the cursor up, down, left and right.

Special Keys

In addition to letters and numbers, the main typing keys also include special keys (Table 4.1). These are Shift, Caps Lock, Tab, Enter, Spacebar, Backspace and Delete.

Table 4.1 *Special keys*

Key	Function
Shift ⇧ Shift	The Shift key is used with other keys for different purposes. We can type a capital letter by pressing Shift key and an alphabet key together. This key is also used to type keys that have more than one symbol on them. ⇧ Shift + G = G ⇧ Shift + * 8 = *
Caps Lock Caps Lock	To type capital letters, press the Caps Lock key. When you want to switch back to small letter typing, press the Caps Lock key again. When the Caps Lock key is turned ON, notice a light on the upper right-hand side of the keyboard. To turn the light OFF, press the key again.
Tab Tab	The Tab key moves the cursor some spaces forward. It is used at the beginning of a new paragraph or to create equal spacing between lines.
Enter Enter	The Enter key is used to start a new line or a paragraph. It moves the cursor to the beginning of a new line.
Spacebar Spacebar	The Spacebar key moves the cursor one space forward. It is used to give space between two words, letters or numbers. It is the longest key on the keyboard.
Backspace ← BackSpace	The Backspace key erases text before the cursor or the selected text.
Delete Delete	The Delete key is used to erase text after the cursor.

Generally, a keyboard has two Enter, Shift, Alt and Ctrl keys.

Soak up!

Do you know there is a way in which we can place our fingers on a keyboard to type faster? Here is the ideal placement of fingers for typing on a keyboard.

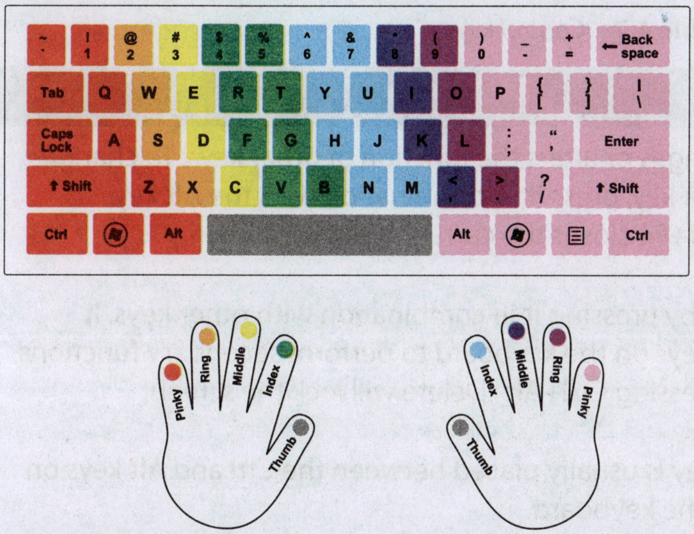

Soak up!

The Delete and Backspace keys help us correct our typing mistakes. The Backspace key erases anything typed to the left of the cursor. The Delete key erases anything typed to the right of the cursor.

Clear up!

Give the results of the following key combinations.

1. ⇧ Shift + L = ____________________

2. ⇧ Shift + ^ 6 = ____________________

3. ⇧ Shift + M (Caps Lock is OFF) = ____________________

4. ⇧ Shift + M (Caps Lock is ON) = ____________________

Control Keys

Control keys are part of the main typing keys (Table 4.2). These keys are used to perform specific actions. The most frequently used control keys are Alt, Ctrl, Windows key and Esc. They can be used alone or in combination with other keys. For example, Pressing "C" while holding down the control key (Ctrl+C) will copy the text.

Table 4.2 *Control keys*

Key	Function
Alt key 	The Alt key changes or alters the function of other keys. To change the function of a key, press it in combination with the Alt key. For example, Alt+F4 closes the current open window.
Ctrl key 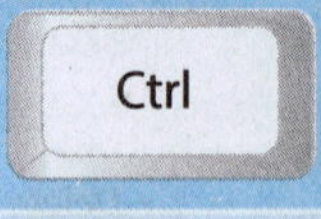	Ctrl key is used by pressing it in combination with other keys. It enables other keys on the keyboard to perform secondary functions. For example, pressing Ctrl+Alt+Delete will lock the screen.
Windows key 	The Windows key is usually placed between the Ctrl and Alt keys on the left side of the keyboard. When pressed alone, it displays the Start screen. When pressed with another key, it does specific functions. For example, when Windows key and L are pressed together, the computer is locked.
Esc 	The Esc key escapes or cancels a task or closes a window. It is also used to stop any running action.

Certain keys are only used in combination with other keys to perform a task. Examples are Shift, Ctrl and Alt keys.

Punctuation Keys

Punctuation keys are mostly located to the right of the letter keys. Examples of punctuation keys are comma (,), full stop (.), colon (:), question mark (?), hyphen (-), quotes (" ") and semicolon (;). Additionally, there are different types of brackets on the keyboard, such as round brackets ( ), curly brackets { } and square brackets [ ]. These keys are used while writing sentences.

Brush up!

Which of the following is not a punctuation mark?

(i) Full stop (.) ☐

(ii) Question mark (?) ☐

(iii) Hashtag symbol (#) ☐

Computer Mouse

A computer mouse is used to:

(i) draw pictures,

(ii) play games,

(iii) watch movies,

(iv) type text, and

(v) select and open applications on the computer screen.

Fig. 4.2 | *A computer mouse*

The arrow on the monitor is called the **mouse pointer**. It moves as we move the mouse. When we type, the shape of the arrow changes to a small blinking line called **cursor**.

Fig. 4.3 | *Mouse pointer and cursor*

> The arrow that appears on the computer screen is called the mouse pointer.
> The small blinking line that appears on the screen while typing is called cursor.

Functions of a Computer Mouse

A mouse has four main parts, as shown in Fig. 4.4.

1. **Left Button**: The left button of the mouse is used for the following three actions:

   a. **Single-click**: Point to a file and click the left button once. Single-clicking on a file will select it. To close an application, left-click once on the cross button.

   b. **Double-click**: The left button is also used to open a file/program or folder. To do this, double-click quickly on it. Double-clicking is mostly used to open items on the desktop.

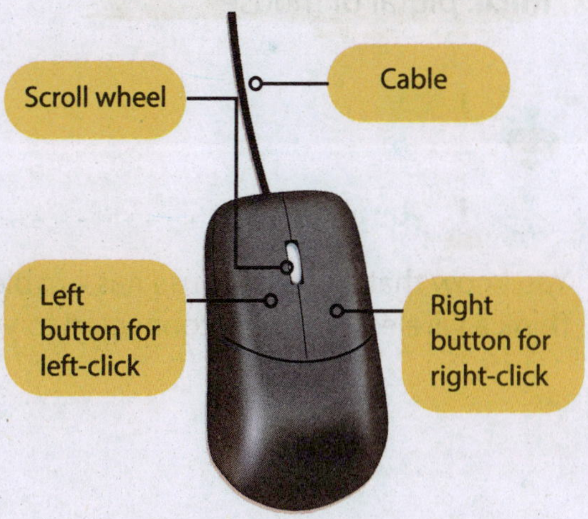

Fig. 4.4 | *Parts of a mouse*

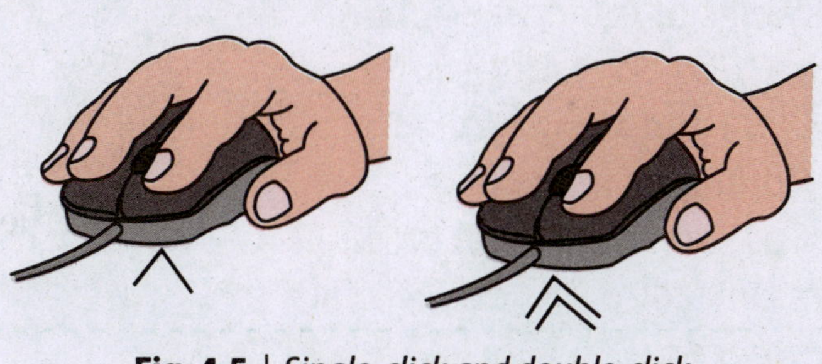

Fig. 4.5 | *Single-click and double-click*

c. **Drag and drop**: We can move items around the screen by dragging and dropping them. It can be done by holding the left button and moving the mouse to drag the selected item. On leaving the left button, the item will get dropped where the cursor points.

drag and drop: select an item and move it to another location on the computer screen

2. **Right button**: The right button is used to get an additional option or a menu with multiple items. To right-click an item, point at the item on the screen and press and release the right button.

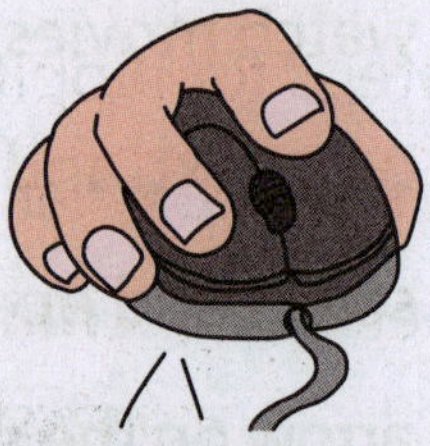

Fig. 4.6 | *Right-click*

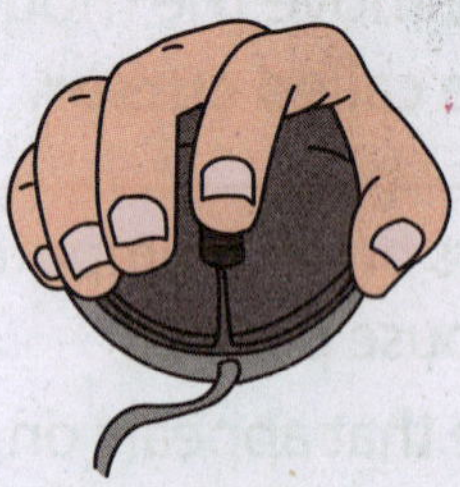

Fig. 4.7 | *Using a scroll wheel*

3. **Scroll wheel**: It is used to move up and down the computer screen. To scroll up, roll the wheel forward. To scroll down, roll the wheel backward.

4. **Cable**: Wired mouse has a long cable that is connected to the CPU. Some mice are available without a cable as well. We call them wireless mice.

mice: plural of mouse

Brush up!

You know that a wired mouse has a cable to connect to the CPU of your computer. How do you think a wireless mouse is connected to your computer? Draw a wireless mouse here.

Flipping the Right and Left Button of the Mouse

Some of us use our left hand for most of the activities. Left-handers can flip the right and left buttons of the mouse.

left-handers: persons who use their left hand rather than their right hand for activities, such as writing and sports and for picking things up

The steps for flipping the mouse button are given below:

1. On the Taskbar, in the search field, type **mouse**.
2. Select the **Change your mouse settings** option.

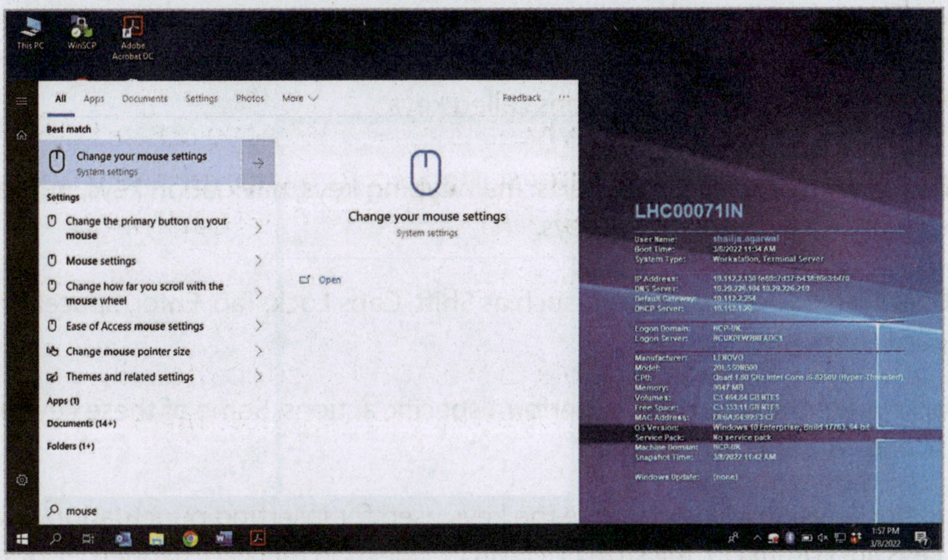

Fig. 4.8 | *Change your mouse settings option in the search results*

3. In the **Settings** window, under **Select your primary button**, change the option in the drop-down list, from **Left** to **Right** or from **Right** to **Left**.

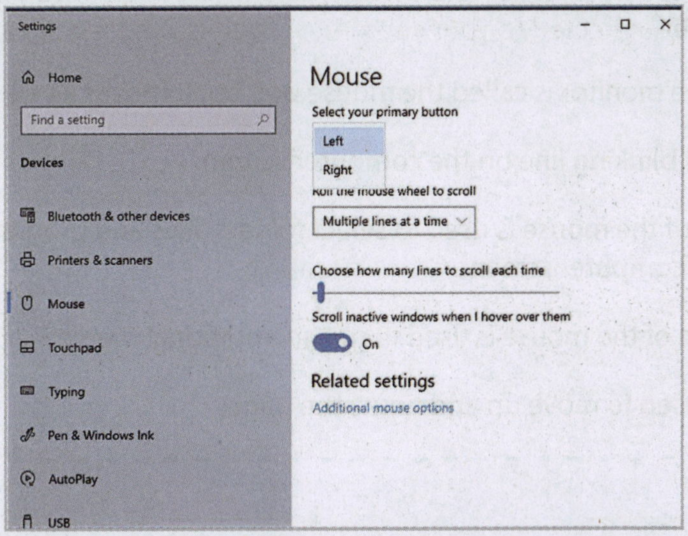

Fig. 4.9 | *Settings window*

Technology Literacy

Crank up!

You can roll the mouse to scroll one screen at a time instead of multiple lines. To do this, in the **Settings window**, go to under **Roll the mouse wheel to scroll** and change the option in the drop-down list from **Multiple lines at a time** to **One screen at a time**.

Today I learned!

- A keyboard has many buttons called keys.
- A keyboard consists of five main parts: main typing keys, navigation keys, numeric keypad, function keys and arrow keys.
- A keyboard has some special keys, such as Shift, Caps Lock, Tab, Enter, Spacebar Backspace, and Delete.
- Control keys are the keys used to perform specific actions. Some of these keys are Alt, Ctrl, Esc and Windows key.
- Punctuation keys on a keyboard are the keys used for inserting punctuation. Examples of these keys are comma (,), full stop (.), colon (:), question mark (?), hyphen (-), quotes (" ") and semicolon (;).
- We can press special key(s) in combination with other keys.
- A mouse helps draw pictures, play games, and select and open applications on the computer screen.
- The arrow on the monitor is called the mouse pointer. It moves as we move the mouse.
- Cursor is a small blinking line on the computer screen.
- The left button of the mouse is used to select folders, files and programs, and drag and drop icons on a computer screen.
- The right button of the mouse is used to get an additional menu.
- Scroll wheel is used to move up and down the page.

Revise and polish!

1. Tick (✓) the correct answer.

a. Which of the following is not a special key?

(i) Tab ☐ (ii) Page Up ☐

(iii) Spacebar ☐ (iv) K ☐

b. Which of the following is not a part of the main typing keys?

(i) Ctrl ☐ (ii) Tab ☐

(iii) Delete ☐ (iv) ⊞ ☐

c. ⇧ Shift + ! 1 gives ____________.

(i) ! sign ☐ (ii) & sign ☐

(iii) # sign ☐ (iv) * ☐

d. Which of the following is not a mouse pointer?

(i)  ☐ (ii)  ☐

(iii)  ☐ (iv)  ☐

e. Select the mouse action used to move up and down the computer screen.

(i) 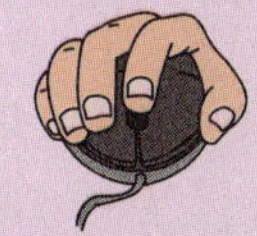 ☐ (ii) 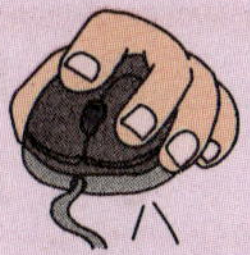 ☐

(iii) 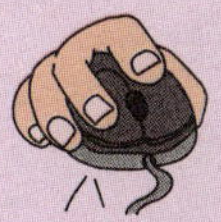 ☐ (iv) 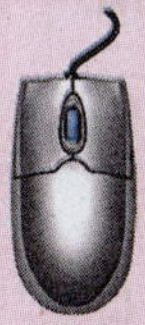 ☐

2. Fill in the blanks using the given words.

right   left   Navigation   special   keys

a. The buttons on a keyboard are called ____________.

b. ____________ keys are used for moving around in documents.

c. The Caps Lock key is a ____________ key.

d. The ____________ button on the mouse is used for double-clicking.

e. The ____________ button is used to get a menu with multiple items.

3. State whether the following statements are true (T) or false (F).

a. The Spacebar key is the longest key on a keyboard. ☐

b. A computer keyboard consists of just alphabet and number keys. ☐

c. The right button of the mouse is used for double-clicking. ☐

d. Left-handers can flip the right and left buttons of the mouse. ☐

e. A wireless mouse comes without a cable. ☐

4. Match the following.

a.	F12	(i)	Special key
b.	Letters	(ii)	Function key
c.	Spacebar	(iii)	Control key
d.	Alt	(iv)	Main typing keys

5. Search the following words in the word grid given below.

Backspace   Shift   Mouse   ALT   Colon

C	S	H	I	F	T	E	R	M
L	E	A	O	Z	S	D	A	O
O	M	O	B	O	T	L	D	U
M	A	J	M	U	S	I	C	S
B	A	C	K	S	P	A	C	E
V	L	A	L	T	O	T	E	K
I	O	M	E	N	E	C	S	L
C	O	L	O	N	D	R	A	W

Lab Activities

Experiential Learning

1. Have you noticed every keyboard in the lab is connected to the computer? Where on the computer is the other side of the wire connected to? Check in the lab and discuss with your friends.

2. With the help of your teacher, learn how to use different keyboard keys. Also, try different key combinations.

3. Open the Notepad program with the help of your teacher. Type your address into it. Now, try doing the following:

   a. Use the Spacebar and the Tab keys in a sentence to add space.

   b. Type capital letters using the Caps Lock and the Shift keys.

   c. Delete a word using the Backspace and the Delete keys.

   Did you notice the difference between the two pair of keys you have used to do the above activities?

4. On the desktop, drag the three icons from the left of the screen and drop them on the centre of the desktop. Write the name of these three icons.

Chapter 5

Introduction to MS Paint

After reading this chapter, I will be able to:

- ✔ Use MS Paint to make drawings.
- ✔ Understand the different features of MS Paint.
- ✔ Explain how to minimize, maximize and close the MS Paint application.

Brainstorm and explore!

Art Integration

Learning Skills

Label the following types of computers and colour them.

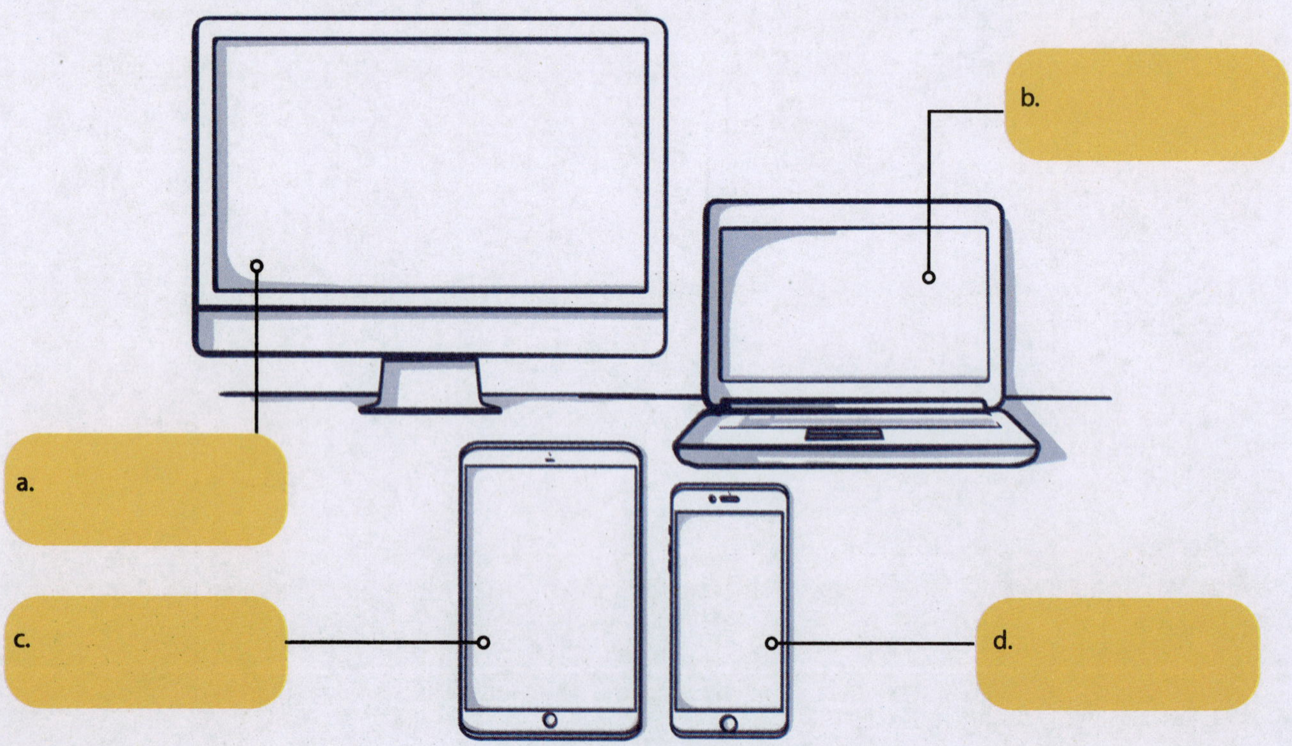

We use tools, such as pencil, eraser, scale and crayons to draw and colour sketches on paper. We can create colourful drawings on the computer as well. The application used for drawing on the computer is MS (Microsoft) Paint. Let us learn how to use MS Paint.

Opening MS Paint

To open MS Paint, follow the steps given below:

1. Click on the **Start** button and type 'MS Paint' in the Search bar on the bottom-left corner of your computer.
2. Click on the **MS Paint** option. The home screen of MS Paint appears (Fig. 5.1).

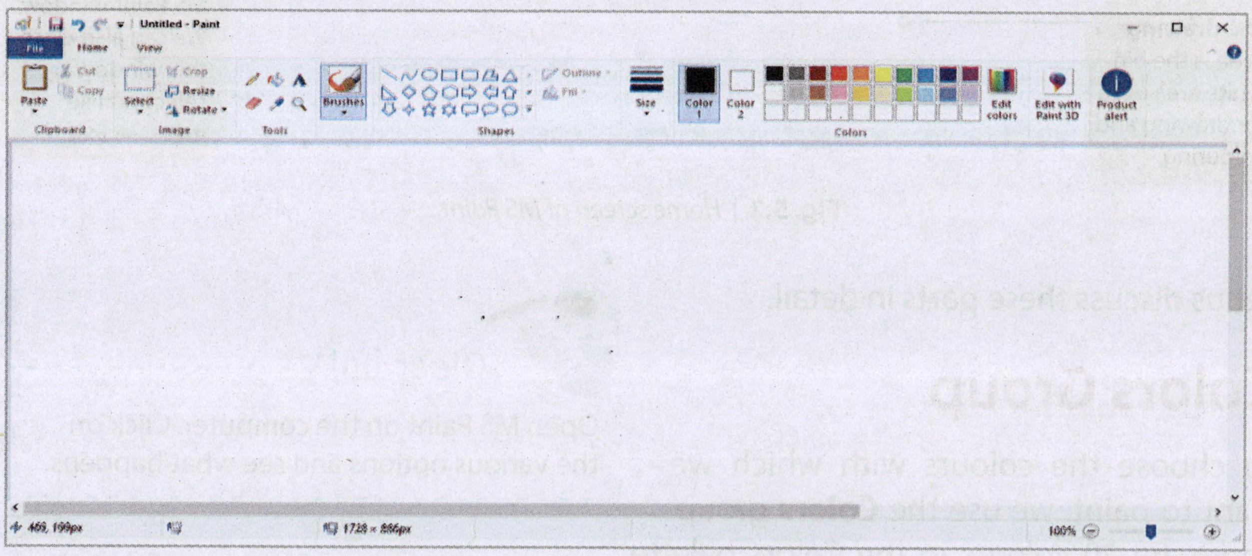

Fig. 5.1 | *Home screen of MS Paint*

Parts of MS Paint Window

The MS Paint window opens with the **File** tab selected. Figure 5.2 shows the basic parts of the MS Paint window.

Crank up!

When we open the MS Paint program, the name of the file is 'Untitled' until we give it a new name.

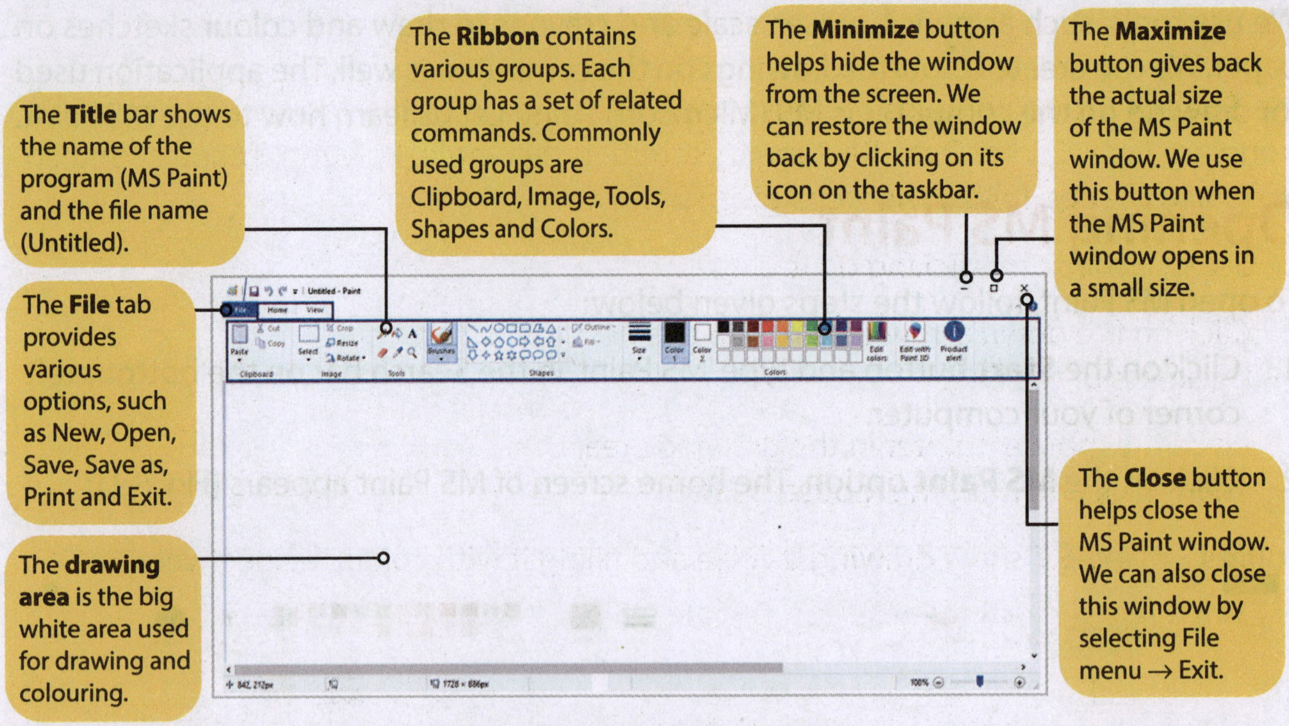

Fig. 5.2 | *Home screen of MS Paint*

Let us discuss these parts in detail.

Clear up!

Open MS Paint on the computer. Click on the various options and see what happens.

Colors Group

To choose the colours with which we want to paint, we use the **Colors** group. There are 20 colours in the Colors palette that can be used to colour a drawing.

The **Edit Colors** option helps select any shade of a colour. When we select this option, a dialog box appears, as shown in Fig. 5.4. After selecting your favourite colour, click on the **OK** button.

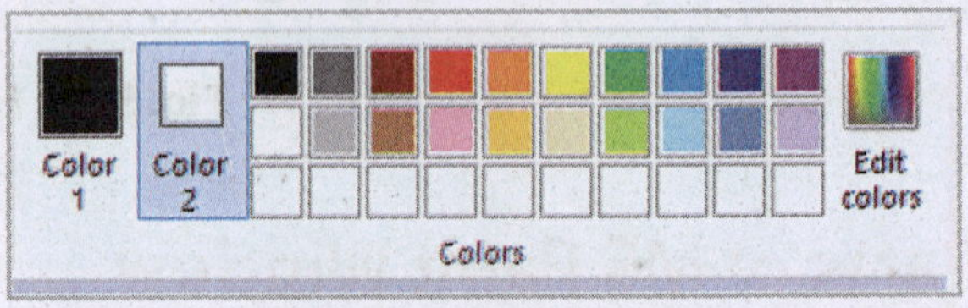

Fig. 5.3 | *Colors palette*

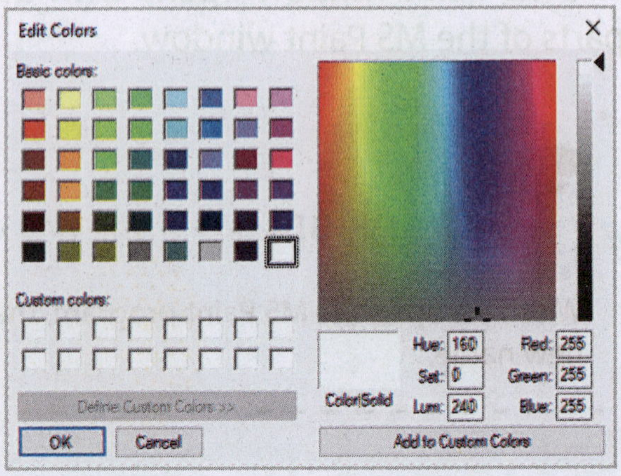

Fig. 5.4 | *Edit Colors dialog box*

Color 1 and Color 2

We can select a foreground colour by clicking on **Color 1** in the **Colors** group and then choosing a colour. We can also select a background colour by clicking on **Color 2** and then choosing a colour.

Shapes Group

The **Shapes** group contains various shape tools. Some of the tools available in this group are Line, Curve, Oval, Rectangle, Rounded rectangle, Polygon, Triangle, and so on. To use Shapes, follow the steps given below:

1. Select a shape by clicking on it.
2. Click on the down arrow below **Size** to select the thickness of the line.
3. Place the mouse pointer in the drawing area. Then, click and drag the mouse pointer.

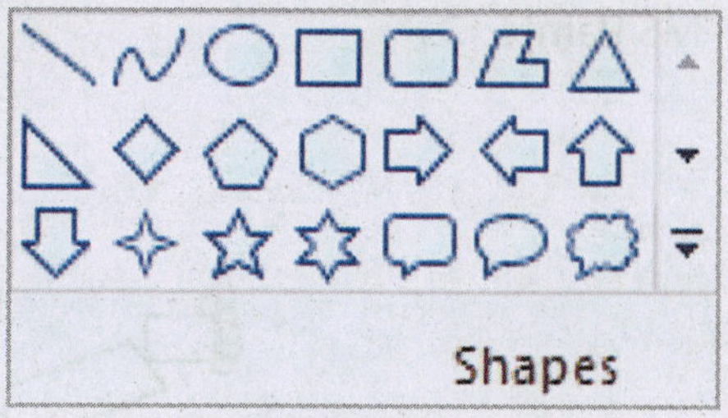

Fig. 5.5 | *Shapes*

Figures 5.6 and 5.7 show drawing a circle and filling it with colour, respectively.

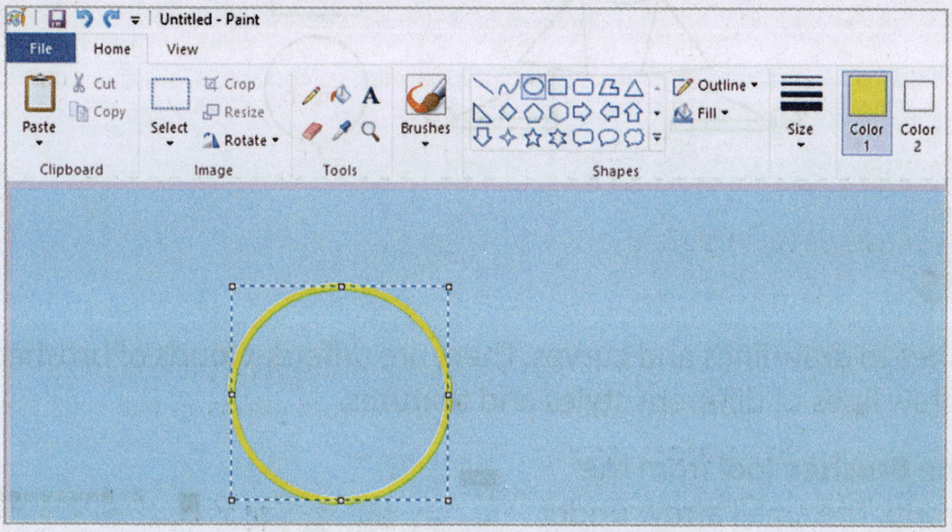

Fig. 5.6 | *Drawing a circle using Shapes*

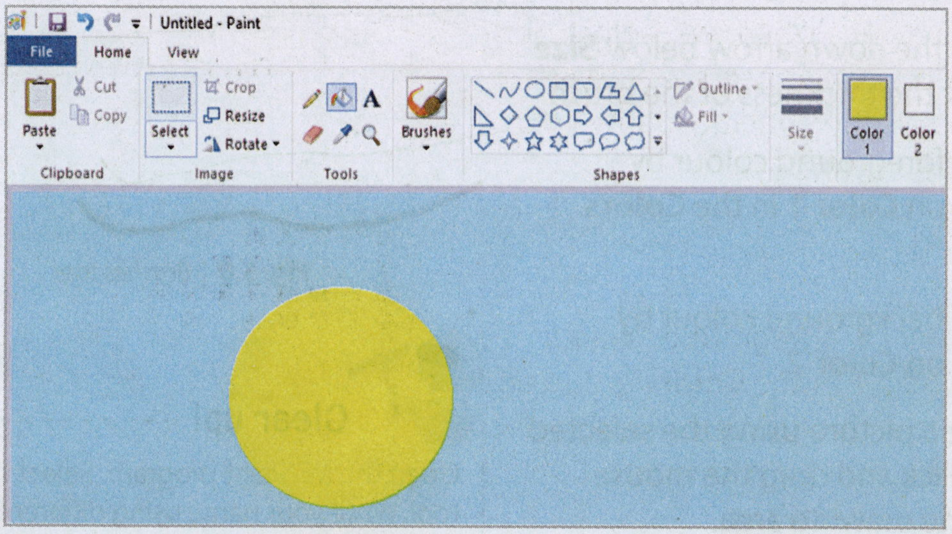

Fig. 5.7 | *Colouring the circle using the Fill with color tool*

Clear up!

Colour the clown as per the colours given for each shape. Can you draw the same using MS Paint?

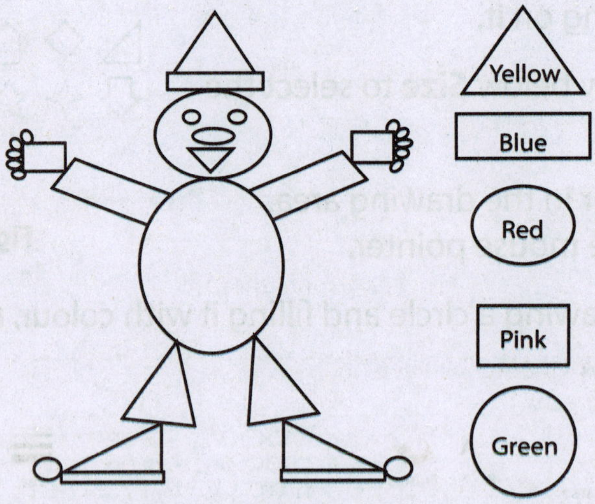

Brushes

We use brushes to draw lines and curves. There are different kinds of brushes. They can be used to draw lines of different styles and textures.

1. Select the **Brushes** tool from the **Tools** group. The small arrow under **Brushes** allows us to select different types of brushes (Fig. 5.8).
2. Click on the down arrow below **Size** to select the thickness of the brush.
3. Select a foreground colour by clicking on **Color 1** in the **Colors** group.
4. Select a background colour by clicking on **Color 2**.
5. To paint a picture using the selected brush, click and drag the mouse inside the drawing area.

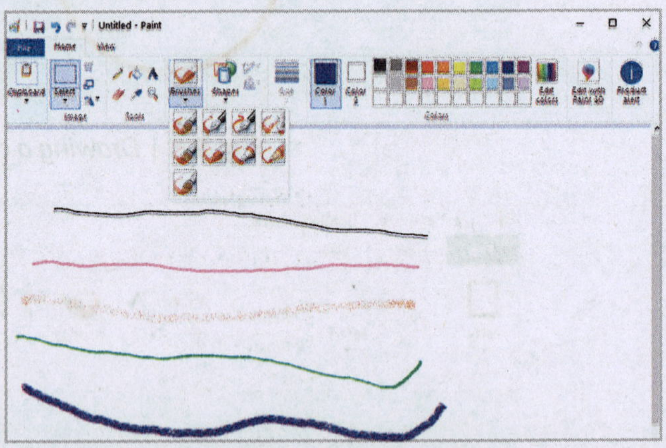

Fig. 5.8 | *Brushes tool*

Clear up!

Open the MS Paint program. Select the Brushes tool. Write your name using different brushes and colours.

Tools Group

The **Tools** group consists of six tools. These tools are discussed below.

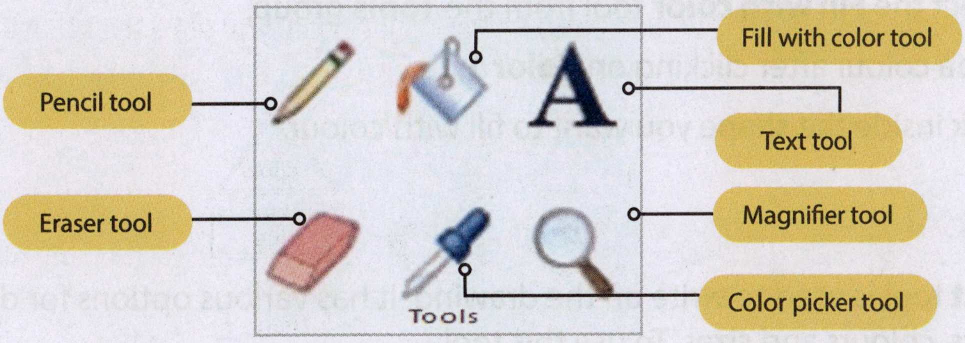

Fig. 5.9 | *Tools group*

Let us learn about the Tools group in detail.

Pencil Tool

The **Pencil** tool is used to draw any shape, just like a real pencil. To use this tool:

1. Select the **Pencil** tool from the **Tools** group.
2. Click on the arrow below **Size** to select the thickness of the line.
3. Select the colour of your choice from the **Colors** group.

Eraser Tool

The **Eraser** tool is used to erase a part or the entire drawing. To use this tool:

1. Select the **Eraser** tool from the Tools group.
2. Select the size of the eraser.
3. Click and drag the mouse pointer over the parts of the image you want to erase.

Color Picker Tool

The **Color picker** tool is used to copy colour from one part of the picture and fill another part with the same colour. To use this tool:

1. Click on the **Color picker** tool from the **Tools** group.
2. Click on the part of the picture from where you want to pick the colour. The picked-up colour will be reflected as **Color 1**.
3. Move the mouse pointer to the part of the picture where you want to apply the same colour. Then, click on it once to apply the same colour.

Fill with color Tool

The **Fill with color** tool is used to colour the background or a shape. For filling colour:

1. Select the **Fill with color** tool from the **Tools** group.
2. Pick a colour after clicking on **Color 1**.
3. Click inside the shape you want to fill with colour.

Text Tool

The **Text** tool is used to write on the drawing. It has various options for different styles of letters, colours and sizes. To use this tool:

1. Click on the **Text** tool.
2. Click on the place in the drawing where the text needs to be placed.
3 Write the desired text.

Magnifier Tool

To magnify or zoom in different parts of the picture, we use the **Magnifier** tool. To use this tool:

1. Click on the **Magnifier** tool.
2. Move the mouse on the part of the image you want to magnify.

Clear up!

1. Open MS Paint and write the following sentence on a green background.

   Nature is beautiful!

   Try the B, I, U options and see what they do.

2. Draw a rainbow using the different tools. Write names of the colours used to draw it.

Creativity

Dan's friends, Aman and Veer, came to his house. After playing for hours together, all of them decided to make drawings with their new crayons. They decided to draw a scenery with a house. After they finished, they saw each other's scenery. Their drawings are shown in Fig. 5.10.

Dan

Aman

Veer

Fig. 5.10 | *Different drawings of sceneries with houses*

Creativity is the use of imagination to make something new.

All of them had to draw a scenery with a house. As their imaginations were different, they created drawings that looked different from each other.

imagination: the part of your mind that allows you to form pictures or the ideas of things that may or may not exist in real life

Creativity is not limited to drawings. There are several ways in which one can be creative.

Buildings

Poems

3D printing

Stories

Fig. 5.11 | *Various kinds of creativity*

Brush up!

Can you draw a building and clouds on a computer? If yes, list the tools and shapes from MS Paint you will use to draw this.

Clear up!

Open the MS Paint program. Select the Text tool. Write your name and school name using different font styles and colours.

Today I learned!

- MS Paint is used to draw and paint on a computer.
- MS Paint drawings, when saved, are stored as images.
- To choose the colours with which we want to paint, we use the Colors palette.
- The Shapes group contains various shapes, such as line, curve, oval, rectangle, rounded rectangle, polygon, triangle, etc.
- The Brushes tool can be used to draw lines of different styles and textures.
- The Pencil tool is used to draw any shape, just like a real pencil.
- The Fill with color tool is used to colour the background or a shape.
- The Text tool is used to write on the drawing.
- The Eraser tool is used to erase a part or the entire drawing.
- The Color picker tool is used to copy colour from one part of the picture and fill another part with the same colour.
- To magnify or zoom-in different parts of the picture, we use the Magnifier tool.
- Creativity is the use of imagination to make something new.
- Creativity is not limited to drawings. There are several ways in which one can be creative.

Revise and polish!

Learning Skills

1. Tick (✓) the correct answer.

a. Which tool do we use to create drawings on a computer?

(i) Pencil ☐ (ii) Crayons ☐

(iii) Sketch pen ☐ (iv) MS Paint ☐

b. Which of the following options is not present under the File tab?

(i) New ☐ (ii) Open ☐

(ii) Save ☐ (iv) Minimize ☐

c. Which option helps select any shade of a colour?

(i) Edit colors ☐ (ii) Format colors ☐

(iii) Print colors ☐ (iv) Check colors ☐

d. Which tool is used to draw any shape?

(i) Triangle ☐ (ii) Oval ☐

(iii) Rectangle ☐ (iv) Pencil ☐

e. Which of the following is not a type of creativity?

(i) Poems ☐ (ii) Drawing ☐

(iii) Stories ☐ (iv) Processing speed ☐

2. Fill in the blanks using the given words.

File Shapes Text Pencil Ribbon

a. The ____________ contains various groups.

b. The ____________ group is used to draw any shape.

c. The ____________ tool is used to write on the drawing.

d. The MS Paint window opens with the ____________ tab selected.

e. We use the ____________ tool to draw lines and curves.

3. State whether the following statements are true (T) or false (F).

a. The Eraser tool is used to erase a part or the entire drawing. ☐

b. The Fill with color tool is used to colour the background or a shape. ☐

c. MS Paint is used to draw and colour documents on computers. ☐

d. The Tools group consists of nine tools. ☐

e. The Edit colors option helps select any shade of a colour. ☐

4. Match the following.

a.	Shapes group	(i)	Pencil tool
b.	Colors group	(ii)	Rectangle tool
c.	Tools group	(iii)	Edit colors option
d.	File tab	(iv)	Shows the program name
e.	Title bar	(v)	Save as option

5. Complete the following table.

S. No.	Task	Tab	Group	Tool
a.	Fill colours to your drawing	File	________	Fill with color
b.	Draw a rectangle	________	Shapes	________
c.	Draw lines and curves	________	Tools	Brushes
d.	Erase a part of your drawing	File	________	Eraser
e.	Write text on your drawing	________	Tools	________

Lab Activities

1. Create the following drawing using MS Paint. List the tools you use to create it.

2. Draw the following pictures with the help of different tools.

a. Ice cream

b. Flower

c. Cat

3. Using the Shapes group, draw the following: Colour the drawing with the colours of your choice. List the shapes you have used.

Chapter

6

Introduction to File Management

After reading this chapter, I will be able to:

- ✔ Define files.
- ✔ Explain the different types of files.
- ✔ Create a file.
- ✔ Discuss how to save and open a file in a computer.

Information Literacy

Brainstorm and explore!

Look at the following images and fill in the missing letters.

1. I_ag_

____

2. _id_o

____

3. D_ _um__nt

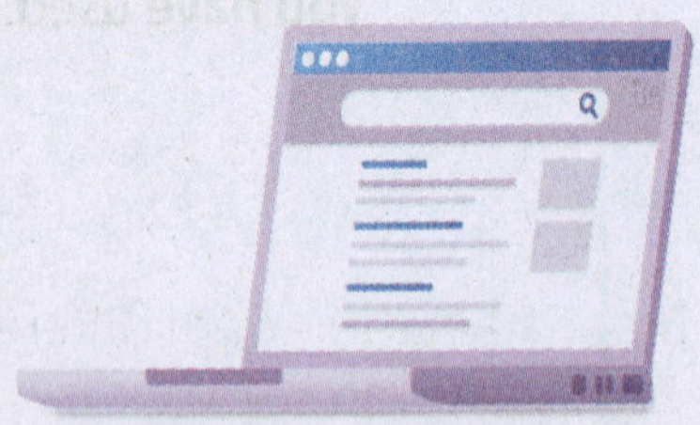

____

In Chapter 1, we learned that data is information processed by or stored in a computer. Do you know how does a computer organize so much data? In computers, data is stored in files and folders. In this chapter, we will learn about data organization in files.

organizing: the process of arranging things in an orderly manner

Files

A file is an object that stores data and information.

There are various types of files available depending on the data stored in it. Each file type can have one or more forms of data, such as images, video, and text.

The most common file types are:

- jpeg/png: Used for pictures/images
- mp4: Used for videos
- doc/docx/txt: Used for text files

A file extension contains of three or four characters (usually letters or numbers). It is added automatically by the computer when we save a file. It is added after a file name. A dot (.) is added before the file extension.

A file can be recognized by its **extension**. Usually, it is written as a full stop (or dot) followed by three/four characters of the file type. For example, a video has the file extension **.mp4**, while images are stored in .jpeg/.png format and GIF images are stored in .gif format.

GIF: a computer file that is used for sending images, specially moving images. GIF is an abbreviation for 'Graphics Interchange Format'.

Crank up!

There are hundreds of different file extensions and file types used in computers. Some of these are given below.

File extension	File type
.doc/.docx/.txt	Text files
.mp4/.mov	Video files
.mp3/.wav	Audio files
.jpeg/.png	Image files

Soak up!

A **folder** is a container where many files can be stored. Folders can also store other folders. A folder within a folder is called a **subfolder**.

Creating a File

To create a text file, right-click anywhere on the screen. Select **New → Text Document**, as shown in Fig. 6.1.

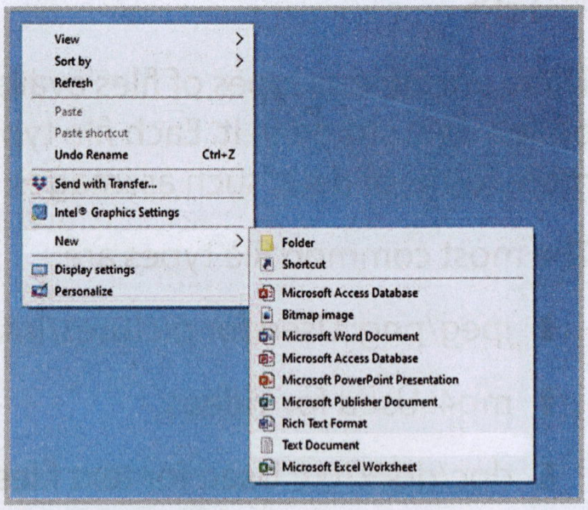

Fig. 6.1 | *Creating a new text file*

Saving a File

In the last chapter, we learned how to create pictures using the MS Paint application. These pictures are all files. To save a file in MS Paint, follow these steps:

1. Open the MS Paint application and create a drawing (Fig. 6.2).

Did you see the name given on the Title bar? It says, "Untitled". This is because the file is not yet saved.

Fig. 6.2 | *Painting created using MS Paint*

2. Go to **File.** A menu will open. Select the **Save as** option (Fig. 6.3).

Since this is an image file, it can be saved in any of the file formats shown in Fig. 6.3. We will click on the PNG picture option to save it as the .png file.

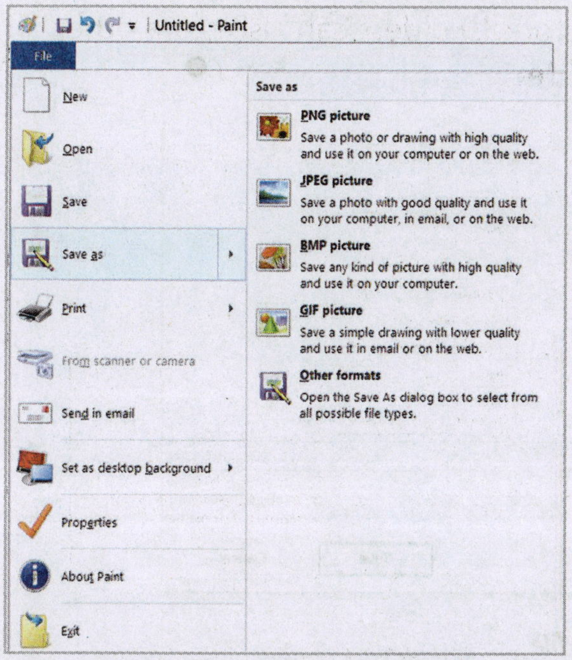

Fig. 6.3 | *Selecting Save as option*

Crank up!

Here are the full forms of some common file extensions:

Extension	Full form
.png	Portable Network Graphics
.jpeg	Joint Photographic Experts Group
.bmp	Bitmap Image File
.gif	Graphics Interchange Format

3. After clicking on **Save as**, a new window (Fig. 6.4) will appear.

Change the filename from Untitled to the name of your choice. Here, we changed it to Smiley.

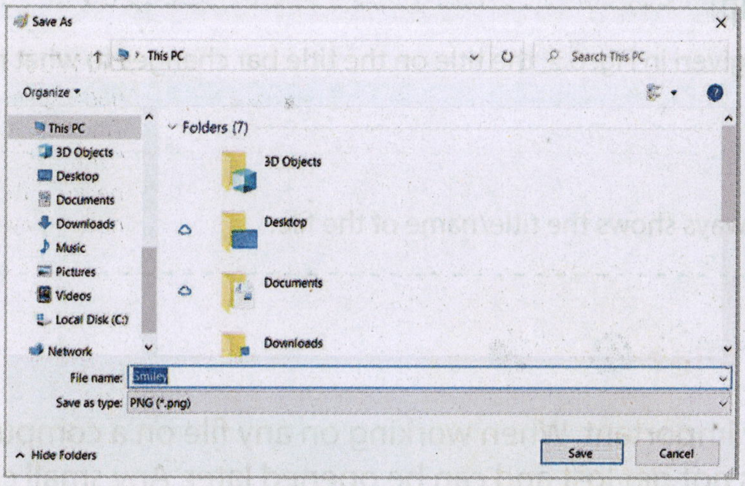

Fig. 6.4 | *Save As window*

4. The File type has been automatically selected as PNG as selected earlier, as shown in Fig. 6.4. We can click on the drop down in the **Save as type** field and change it to any other type as well.

5. The file can be saved anywhere on the computer. If you click on the Desktop, the file gets saved on the desktop of the computer.

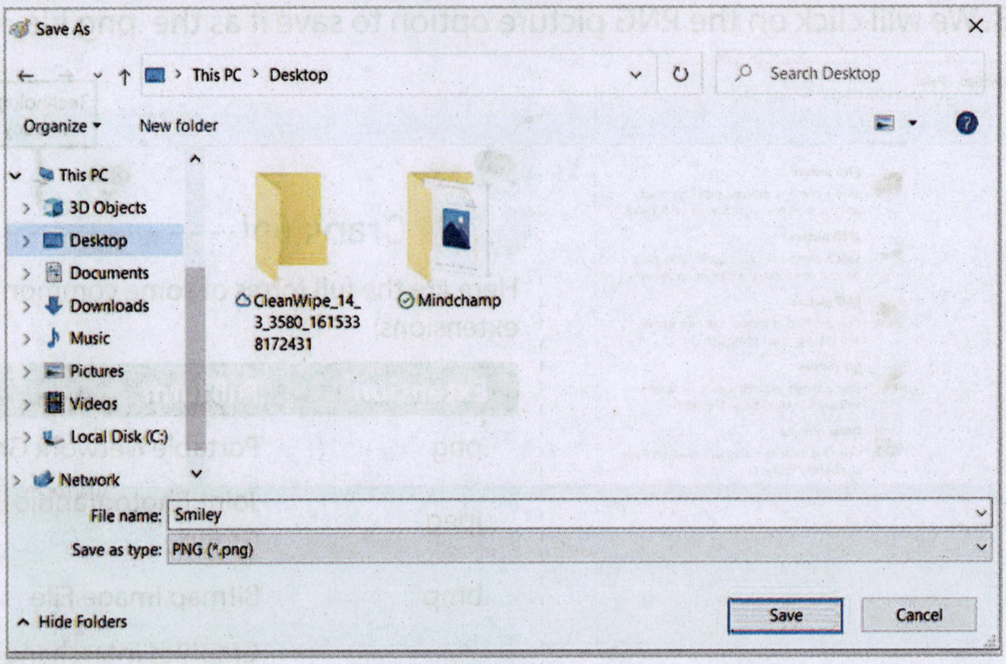

Fig. 6.5 | *Saving a file*

6. Click on the **Save** button to save the file Smiley.png on the desktop (Fig. 6.5).

Brush up!

After saving the file given in Fig. 6.2, the title on the title bar changes to what name?

____

Hint: The title bar always shows the title/name of the file.

Why to Save a File?

Saving a file is very important. When working on any file on a computer, always save it. A saved file does not get lost and can be opened later. Any small change made to the file needs to be saved; else, it will get erased.

By saving a file, we can keep the file for future use. A saved file can be shared with others.

A file can be saved anywhere on the computer.

Opening a File

We can open an already saved file (Fig. 6.6). To do this, double-click on it. The saved file will open.

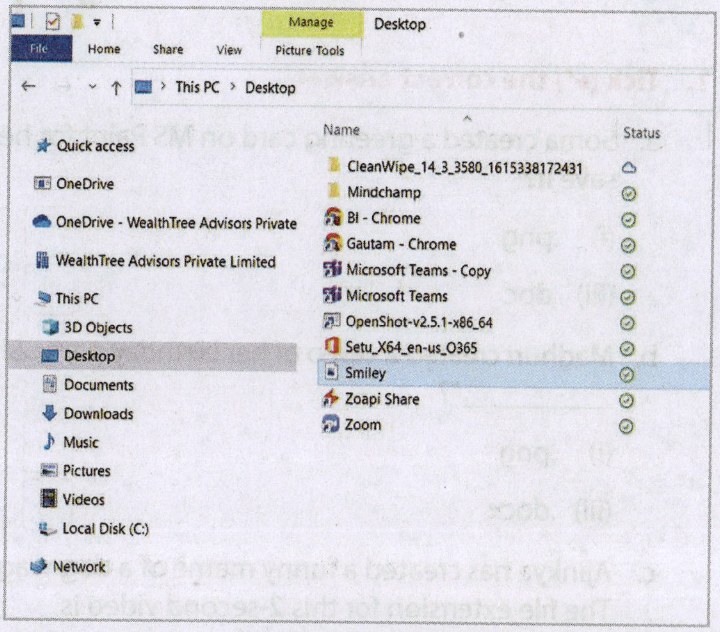

Fig. 6.6 | *Opening a file*

Clear up!

Circle the option that is used to close the application window.

Hint: We have used it in the MS Paint file in the last chapter.

Soak up!

- The keyboard shortcut to save a file is Ctrl+S.
- The keyboard shortcut to open a file is Ctrl+O.

Today I learned!

- We should always store all the data in a computer neatly, using files and folders, so that they can be easily found later.
- A file stores data and information, while a folder organizes the files in a group.
- There are various types of files available, depending on the data to be stored in it.
- A file extension is added to the end of a filename. It tells us what type of file is being used.
- Any small change made to the file needs to be saved, else it will get erased.
- A file can be saved using the Save as button.
- The file can be saved anywhere on the computer.
- We can open an already saved file by double-clicking on it.

Revise and polish!

Learning Skills

1. Tick (✔) the correct answer.

a. Soma created a greeting card on MS Paint for her son. What file extension will she use to save it?

(i) .png ☐ (ii) .mp4 ☐

(iii) .doc ☐ (iv) .txt ☐

b. Madhuri created a video of her birthday party. She can save the video as "my birthday. __________"?

(i) .png ☐ (ii) .mp4 ☐

(iii) .docx ☐ (iv) .jpeg ☐

c. Ajinkya has created a funny meme of a dog wagging his tail. He shares it with all his friends. The file extension for this 2-second video is __________.

(i) .GIF ☐ (ii) .mp4 ☐

(iii) .doc ☐ (iv) .txt ☐

d. Sneha typed a letter for her mother on the computer. Select the correct file extension of this letter.

(i) .txt ☐ (ii) .gif ☐

(iii) .png ☐ (iv) .mp4 ☐

e. Aju has clicked a lot of pictures and videos on his phone for his wedding. Which of the following files are not pictures?

(i) Files with extension .png ☐ (ii) Files with extension .jpeg ☐

(iii) Files with extension .mp4 ☐ (iv) Files with extension .bmp ☐

2. Fill in the blanks using the words given below.

Save as extension mp4 folder erased

a. Video files are stored in the __________ format.

b. A file can be saved using the __________ button.

c. A file type can usually be recognized by its __________.

d. A file can get __________ if not saved.

e. A __________ is a container where many files can be stored.

3. **State whether the following statements are true (T) or false (F).**

a. Any small change made to a file needs to be saved, else it will get erased. ☐

b. A folder in a computer is an object that stores data and information. ☐

c. A file extension is the start of a filename. ☐

d. To save a file, we need to click on the Print button. ☐

e. A file can only be saved on the Desktop. ☐

4. **Match the following.**

a.	Save as	(i)	Extension of a text file
b.	.jpeg	(ii)	Extension of a picture file
c.	.mp4	(iii)	Stores data in a computer
d.	Files	(iv)	Extension of a video
e.	.txt files	(v)	To save files

5. **Give the names of any four file types.**

a. ____________________ b. ____________________

c. ____________________ d. ____________________

Lab Activities

1. Go to the lab and switch ON the computer. Make a list of different types of files present on the computer.
2. Shailja needs to write an essay on an animal.

   Take the help of your teacher to open the Notepad application. Help Shailja by typing a 10-line essay describing your favourite animal. Make sure you save the file so that you can share it with Shailja later.

   What will be the file extension of this file?
3. Create a drawing using MS Paint and save it on the desktop of your computer lab.

Art Integration

Learning Skills

Worksheet 1 (Chapters 1 and 2)

1. Colour the features of computers in red and those of humans in blue.

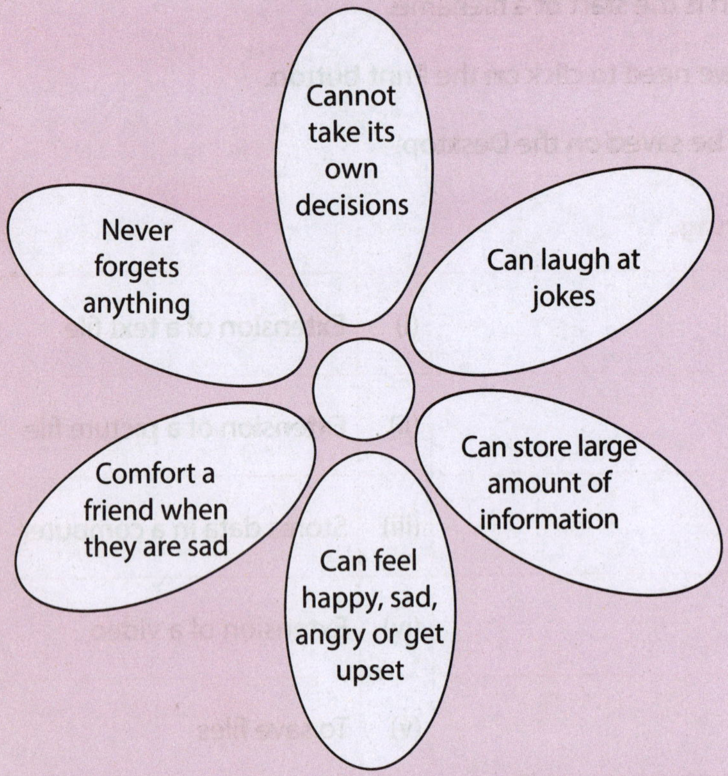

2. Tick (✓) the correct answer.

a. Which of the following places do not use computers?

(i) Classroom ☐ (ii) Office ☐

(iii) Garden ☐ (iv) Railway station ☐

b. Who of the following cannot be a user of computers?

(i) Student ☐ (ii) Teacher ☐ (iii) Principal ☐ (iv) Plants ☐

c. What is multitasking?

(i) Doing one thing at a time ☐ (ii) Doing nothing at a time ☐

(iii) Doing many things at a time ☐ (iv) Taking decisions ☐

d. At which place is computers are used to deposit money?

(i) Office ☐ (ii) School ☐ (iii) Home ☐ (iv) Bank ☐

e. Who launches rockets using computers?

(i) Architects ☐ (ii) Doctors ☐ (iii) Scientists ☐ (iv) Teachers ☐

Art Integration

Learning Skills

Worksheet 2 (Chapters 3 and 4)

1. In the following picture, colour the keys that make the name of your school.

2. Name the following things as input or output.

a.	 ____________	 ____________
b.	 ____________	 ____________
c.	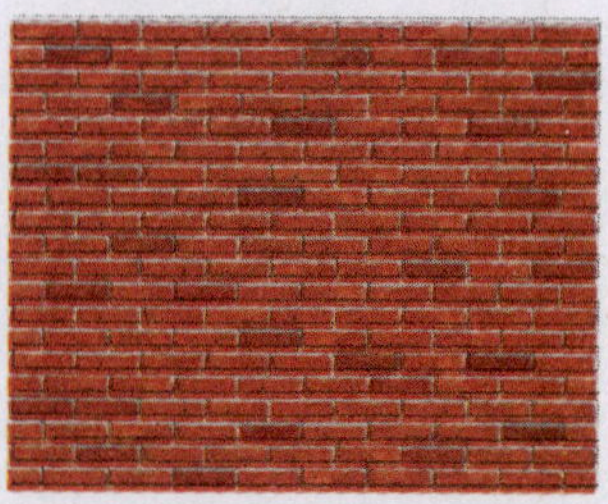 ____________	 ____________

Worksheet 3 (Chapters 5 and 6)

1. Colour, count and write the number of each shape.

☆ yellow	○ green	□ pink

☆	○	□

2. Match the following file types with the correct extension.

a.	 Music	(i)	.mp4
b.	 Documents	(ii)	.mp3
c.	 Videos	(iii)	.doc

Additional Worksheet

1. **Circle the image in which a particular shape is present in an ordered, repetitive manner. Cross the ones with no particular order.**

a.	 A four-leaf clover	 Waterfall
b.	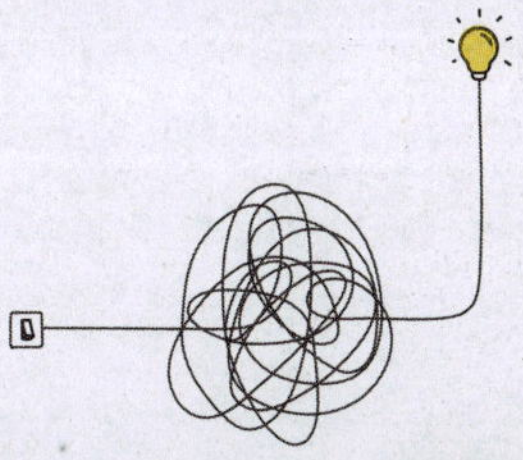 Tangled wires	 Brick wall

2. **The repeated parts that make up a pattern are called motifs. Draw the motifs that make up the following patterns. One has been done for you.**

a.  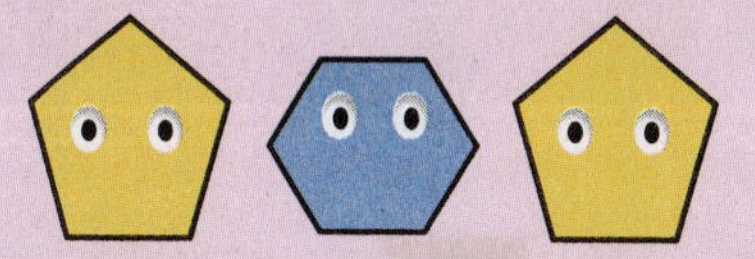

b. 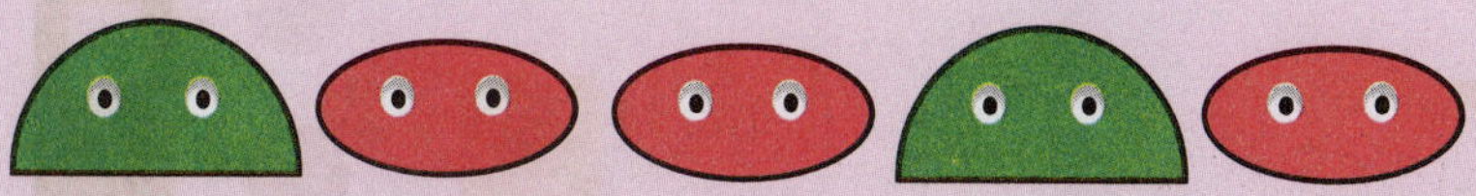 ____________________

c.  ____________________

d. 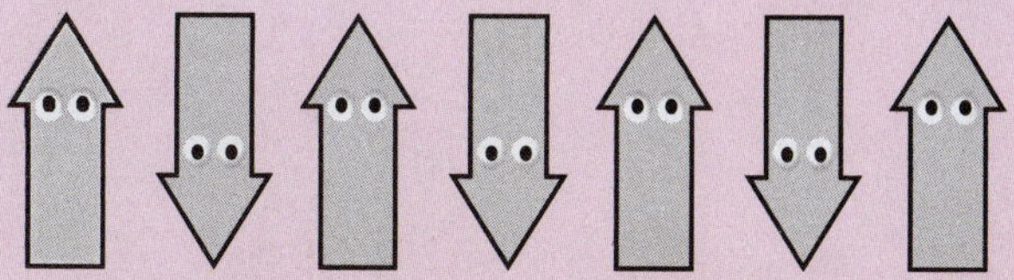 ____________________

e.  ____________________

Fun Activity

Look at the following picture. Tick (✓) the correct set of shapes that is used to make the vehicle in the centre.

CLASS 2

QUESTION PAPER SET A

NCO

SOF NATIONAL CYBER OLYMPIAD 2021-22

DO NOT OPEN THIS BOOKLET UNTIL ASKED TO DO SO

Total Questions: 35 | Time: 1 hr.

Guidelines for the Candidate

1. You will get additional ten minutes to fill up information about yourself on the OMR Sheet, before the start of the exam.
2. Write your **Name, School Code, Class, Roll No.** and **Mobile Number** clearly on the **OMR Sheet** and do not forget to sign it. We will share your marks / result and other information related to SOF exams on your mobile number.
3. The Question Paper comprises three sections:

   Logical Reasoning (5 Questions), **Computers and Information Technology** (25 Questions) and **Achievers Section** (5 Questions).

   Each question in Achievers Section carries 2 marks, whereas all other questions carry one mark each.
4. All questions are compulsory. There is no negative marking. Use of calculator is not permitted.
5. There is only ONE correct answer. Choose only ONE option for an answer.
6. To mark your choice of answers by darkening the circles on the OMR Sheet, use **HB Pencil** or **Blue / Black ball point pen** only. E.g.

   Q.16: _____ means to hold down the left mouse button while you move the mouse pointer to a new place.

   A. Single click B. Double click C. Dragging D. Left click

   As the correct answer is option C, you must darken the circle corresponding to option C on the OMR Sheet. 16. Ⓐ Ⓑ ● Ⓓ
7. Rough work should be done in the blank space provided in this booklet.
8. Return the OMR Sheet to the invigilator at the end of the exam.
9. Please fill in your personal details in the space provided on this page before attempting the paper.

SOF

SCIENCE OLYMPIAD FOUNDATION

Inspiring Young Minds Through Knowledge Olympiads

Name:..

SOF Olympiad Roll No.:.. Contact No.:..

1. Which of the following is the heaviest?

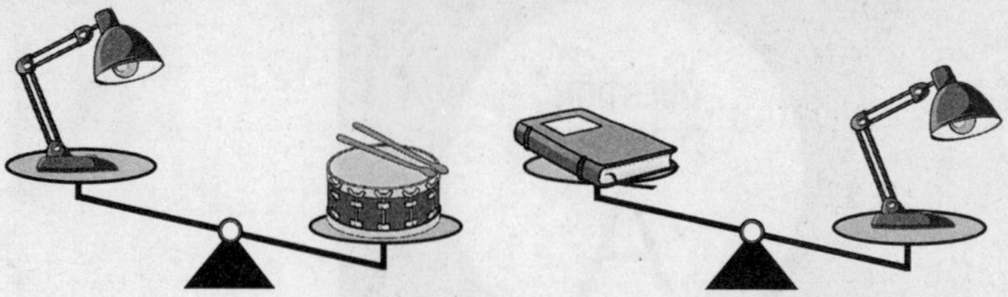

A. 

B. 

C. 

D. Can't be determined

2. Select the odd one out.

A. 

B. 

C. 

D. 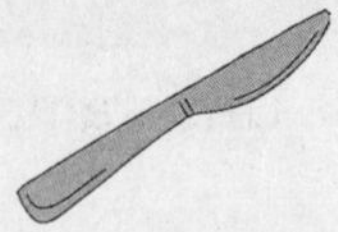

3. Which of the following figures will complete the given figure pattern?

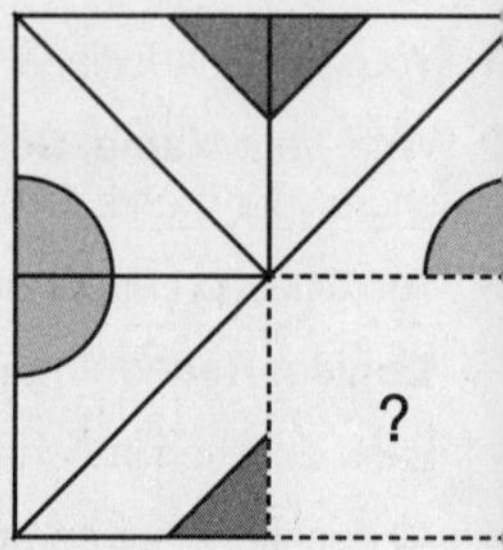

A. 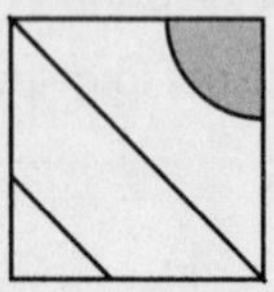

B. 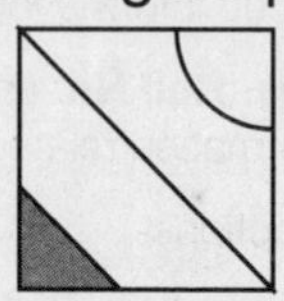

C. 

D. 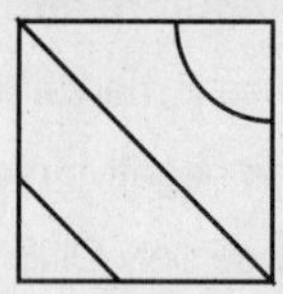

4. Which of the following items costs the least?

A. 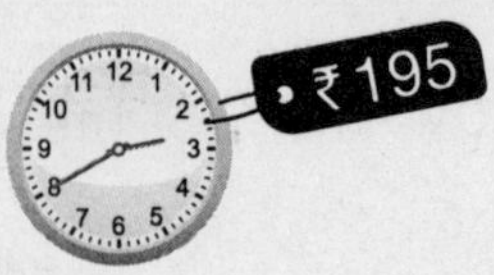

B. 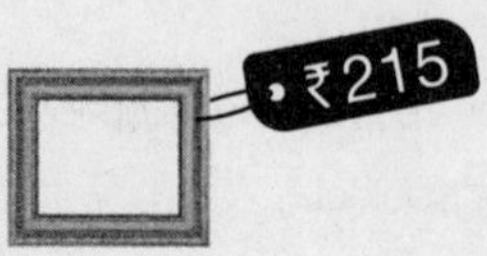

C. 

D. 

5. If pen stand M and R are removed from the given arrangement, then pen stand ______ is third from the right end.

(Left) W S J L R P T M U V

A. T B. L C. J D. M

SPACE FOR ROUGH WORK

6. Computers at the shown place can be used to ________.

A. Generate bill for purchased items

B. Keep the details of patients

C. Send rockets into space

D. Print newspapers

---

7. A computer can perform the tasks of which of the following devices?

A. 

B. 

C. 

D. 

---

8. Unscramble the given letters and select the CORRECT use of computer at that place.

OLHSCO

A. To solve sums

B. To play video games

C. To print passbooks

D. To deposit checks

---

9. Select the CORRECT statement about computers.

A. It does not get bored doing the same work again and again.

B. It cannot work as fast as humans.

C. It cannot store information.

D. It has feelings.

---

10. Which of the following options contains the features such as built-in keyboard, microphone, speaker, etc.?

A. 

B. 

C. 

D. 

---

11. To shut down a computer, you should first click on ________.

A. 

B. 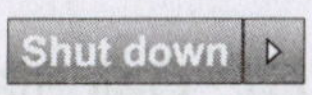

C. 

D. 

SPACE FOR ROUGH WORK

12. How many types of keys names of keyboard are hidden in the given word grid?

S	A	Z	E
H	D	X	N
I	I	Y	T
F	J	R	E
T	A	B	R
C	L	Q	O

A. 3
B. 4
C. 5
D. 1

---

13. Which of the following parts of computer can be moved along the hard, flat surface to control the cursor position on monitor screen?

A. Keyboard B. CPU C. Printer D. Mouse

---

14. The given image shows the ________ operation of a mouse and it allows to ________.

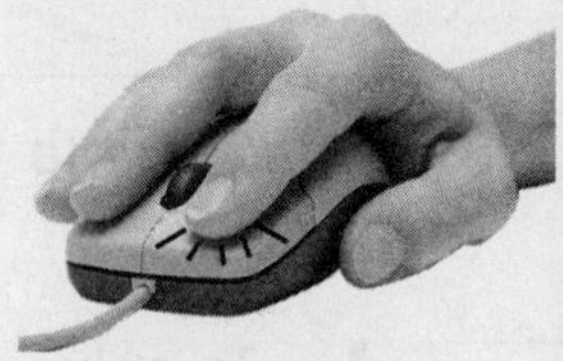

A. Left-click, select an object on screen
B. Right-click, select an object on screen
C. Left-click, open a short menu for the selected object
D. Right-click, open a short menu for the selected object

---

15. Which of the following letters when unscrambled, describes one of the characteristics of computer?

A. RATSM B. LUDL C. WLOS D. MUDB

---

16. At airport and railway stations, computers can be used for ________.

A. Opening a new bank account
B. Displaying arrival and departure of flights and trains
C. Designing building, houses and flyovers
D. Printing newspapers

---

17. Which of the following is INCORRECT about computer?

A. It can do very large calculations in few seconds.
B. It can store very large amount of data.
C. It allows you to get in touch with your friends by means of video calling.
D. It cannot work for long hours.

---

18. The result of any calculations done on computer can be seen on a monitor. A monitor is also known as ____________.

A. Visual display unit B. Calculation device
C. Resultant unit D. Graphical device

SPACE FOR ROUGH WORK

19. Which of the following devices will replace the '?' and prints the flower shown on the monitor screen onto the piece of paper?

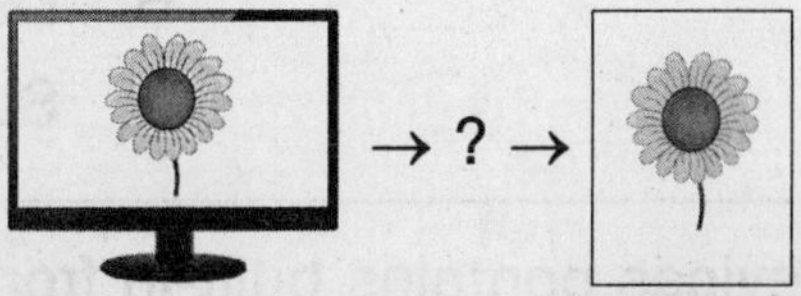

A. 

B. 

C. 

D. 

---

20. Which of the following devices can be used to record video at home or offices for security purpose?

A. 

B. 

C. 

D. 

---

21. Sujata wants to move some icons from their current locations to new locations. On computer which of the following devices she can use?

A. 

B. 

C. 

D. 

---

22. Which of the following devices can be used to play the game shown here?

A. 

B. 

C. 

D. 

---

23. Which of the following keys is NOT found on a computer keyboard?

A. 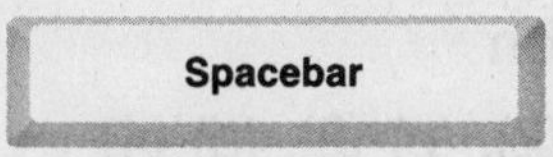

B. 

C. 

D. 

SPACE FOR ROUGH WORK

24. Which of the following can be considered as a hand-held computer?

A. Tablet
B. Desktop
C. Mainframe
D. Super

25. Which of the following devices contains built-in front-facing camera that is used to ta selfies?

A. Smartphones
B. Desktop
C. Keyboard
D. Printer

26. Which of the following statements is CORRECT about the keyboard key shown in t given image?

A. When pressed, it sends cursor to the beginning of the previous line.
B. This key is generally available two times on a standard keyboard and both of the performs same tasks.
C. In an opened dialog box, it is used to stop the ongoing action.
D. It is used to type all the letters in capital.

27. Using  tool, you can create free hand drawings in MS-Paint. Which of the followi options represents the use of this tool?

A. 
B. 
C. 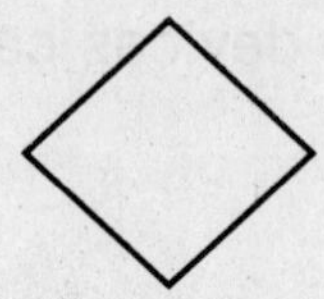
D. 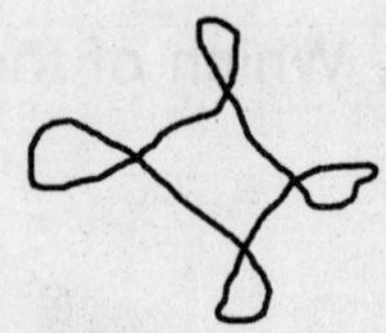

28. Match the parts of computers given in Column-1 with their relevant tasks given Column-2.

Column-1	Column-2
(a) CPU	(1) Typing
(b) Monitor	(2) Pointing
(c) Keyboard	(3) Display
(d) Mouse	(4) Computation

A. (a)-(4), (b)-(3), (c)-(1), (d)-(2)
B. (a)-(1), (b)-(2), (c)-(3), (d)-(4)
C. (a)-(4), (b)-(3), (c)-(2), (d)-(1)
D. (a)-(2), (b)-(4), (c)-(3), (d)-(1)

SPACE FOR ROUGH WORK

29. It is the processing unit of a computer. All major activities of the computer are coordinated by this part of the computer. Identify it.

A. 
B. 
C. 
D. 

30. The given image is of ____________.

A. A computer hardware
B. A music video app
C. A mobile gaming app
D. A set of pokemon images who get angry with anyone who watch them

ACHIEVERS SECTION

31. Which of the following options will allow you to select the part of the drawing as shown in the given image in MS-Paint?

A. 
B. 
C. 
D. 

32. Anisha is having a device placed on top of the computer monitor screen that allows her to record video. Which of the following types of device is Anisha using?

A. 
B. 
C. 
D. 

33. Unscramble the given letters and identify the part of computer related to it.

ESSNHTIGRB

A. 
B. 
C. 
D. 

SPACE FOR ROUGH WORK

34. How many application areas of computer are hidden in the given word grid?

P	O	L	I	C	E	E	Z
A	H	E	Q	P	Z	Z	Y
D	E	F	E	N	C	E	B
F	G	K	L	O	Y	I	U
M	I	L	I	T	A	R	Y

A. 3 B. 4 C. 2 D. 5

35. Select the INCORRECT match regarding the given keys with their actions.

A. Caps Lock + D → D

B. ⇧ Shift + &/7 → &

C. !/1 + @/2 → 12

D. ⇧ Shift +)/7 → 0

SPACE FOR ROUGH WORK

ANSWER KEYS

1.	(C)	**2.**	(D)	**3.**	(C)	**4.**	(C)	**5.**	(A)	**6.**	(A)	**7.**	(A)
8.	(A)	**9.**	(A)	**10.**	(A)	**11.**	(A)	**12.**	(A)	**13.**	(D)	**14.**	(A)
15.	(A)	**16.**	(B)	**17.**	(D)	**18.**	(A)	**19.**	(D)	**20.**	(B)	**21.**	(A)
22.	(A)	**23.**	(D)	**24.**	(A)	**25.**	(A)	**26.**	(B)	**27.**	(D)	**28.**	(A)
29.	(A)	**30.**	(C)	**31.**	(B)	**32.**	(C)	**33.**	(A)	**34.**	(A)	**35.**	(D)

SOF SCIENCE OLYMPIAD FOUNDATION

National Office: Plot 99, First Floor, Sector 44 Institutional area, Gurugram -122 003 (HR) India

Email: info@sofworld.org | Website: www.sofworld.org

Regd. Office: 406, Taj Apt., Ring Road, New Delhi-110 029

Note: Please address all communication to the National Office only.

NOTES

NOTES